THE
SOMERSET & DORSET
RAILWAY
1935–1966

On a sunny late afternoon, former Midland Railway 4-4-0 Class '2P' No. 40505 climbs away southwards from Midsomer Norton and heads towards Chilcompton Tunnel with the 4.35pm Bath to Templecombe stopping train. This was a location which, from 1950, Norman Lockett revisited time and time again and, judging from this picture, who could blame him! Notice how the exhaust of No. 40505 is snatched away by the strong sou'westerly wind on this exposed section along the flank of Norton Down. *15th July 1953*

Class '2P' 4-4-0 No. 40563 assists Stanier 'Black Five' No. 44830 with the down 'Pines Express', having left Bath (former Midland Railway) station just 7 to 8 minutes earlier. The gradient is 1 in 50 and, on emerging from Devonshire Tunnel, both locomotives make their presence heard in no uncertain manner whilst passing through Lyncombe Vale, heading towards the summit of the climb on the approach to Combe Down Tunnel. *23rd May 1951*

THE
SOMERSET & DORSET
RAILWAY
1935-1966

MIKE ARLETT & DAVID LOCKETT

Lightmoor Press

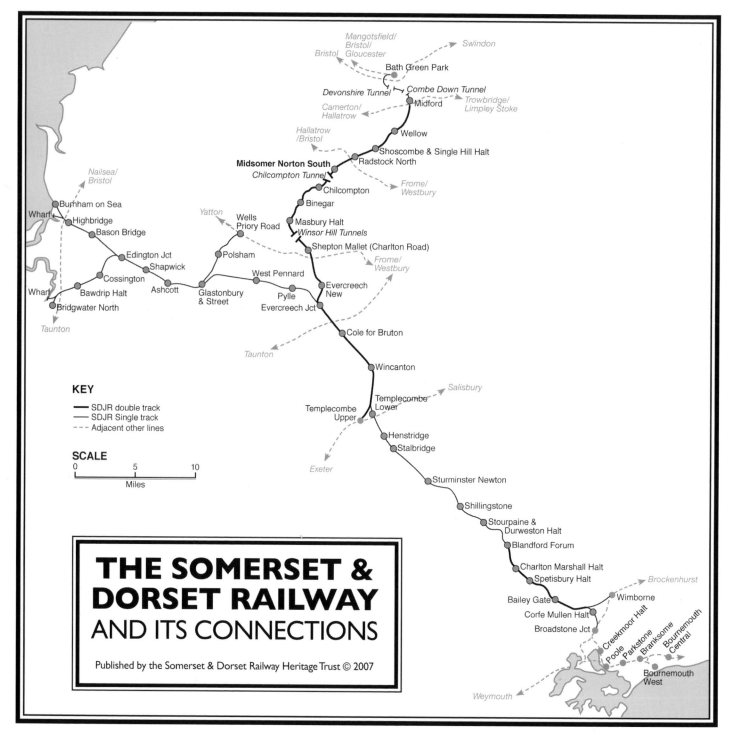

THE SOMERSET & DORSET RAILWAY
AND ITS CONNECTIONS

Published by the Somerset & Dorset Railway Heritage Trust © 2007

KEY

— SDJR double track
— SDJR Single track
--- Adjacent other lines

SCALE

0   5   10
Miles

Published by LIGHTMOOR PRESS
© Lightmoor Press, Mike Arlett & David Lockett
Designed by Mike Arlett & Neil Parkhouse
Revised Second Edition May 2010
British Library Cataloguing-in-Publication Data. A catalogue record for this book is available from the British Library
ISBN 13: 9781899889 31 0

LIGHTMOOR PRESS
Unit 144B, Lydney Trading Estate, Harbour Road, Lydney, Gloucestershire GL15 5EJ
www.lightmoor.co.uk
Lightmoor Press is an imprint of Black Dwarf Lightmoor Publications Ltd

Printed & bound by TJ International, Padstow, Cornwall

THE NORMAN LOCKETT ARCHIVE

CONTENTS

FOREWORD ... PAGE 7

INTRODUCTION ... PAGE 8

ACKNOWLEDGEMENTS ... PAGE 9

THE HISTORICAL BIT ... PAGE 11

SECTION 1:

THE 1930s: A FIRST VISIT TO THE S&D ... PAGE 13

✤ 1930s MOTIVE POWER ✤ THE CLASS '7F' 2-8-0s (1914 SERIES) ✤ 1938 ANCIENT & MODERN ✤

SECTION 2:

POST WAR 1940s: THE END OF THE GROUPING ... PAGE 25

✤ AUTUMN AROUND WELLOW ✤ AN AFTERNOON AT MIDFORD 28TH MAY 1947 ✤ A 'BLACK FIVE' WITH THE 'PINES' ✤
✤ THE END OF AN ERA ... ✤ ... AND THE START OF ANOTHER ✤

SECTION 3:

1948 TO 1952: NATIONALISATION – AND SOME RATIONALISATION ... PAGE 37

✤ THE 'CLEETHORPES' ✤ WINSOR HILL ✤ IN & OUT OF COMBE DOWN TUNNEL ✤ SOUTH OF MIDSOMER NORTON ✤
✤ REDAN BRIDGE ✤ MAIN LINE FREIGHT ✤ BRANCH LINE FREIGHT ✤ RETURN TO HIGHBRIDGE ✤ BURNHAM ✤
✤ HIGHBRIDGE CHURCH STREET CROSSING ✤ OUT AND BACK ✤ FREIGHT TO THE WHARF ✤ COAL FOR BURNHAM ✤
✤ NEWBRIDGE ACCOMMODATION CROSSING ✤ THE BRIDGWATER BRANCH OCTOBER 1951 ✤ 'THE PINES EXPRESS' ✤
✤ THE S&D CLASS '7F' 2-8-0s (1925 SERIES) ✤ TUCKING MILL ✤ MOTIVE POWER ANCIENT AND MODERN ✤
✤ SOME OLD FAVOURITES ✤ FIRST SIGNS OF A NEW REGIME ✤ AFTERNOON LOCALS ✤ JOINT EFFORT ON A JOINT LINE! ✤

SECTION 4:

1953 TO 1957: FIVE HALCYON YEARS FOR THE LINESIDE OBSERVER ... PAGE 87

✤ MASBURY SUMMIT ✤ 'TI' EXCURSION ✤ CLOSURE OF A LITTLE KNOWN S&D OUTPOST ✤
✤ THE BR STANDARD CLASS '5' 4-6-0s COME TO THE S&D ✤ DEVONSHIRE BANK ✤ TEMPLECOMBE 'TRANSFER' ✤
✤ THE VERSATILE CLASS '4F' 0-6-0s ✤ SOME ELDERLY MOTIVE POWER ✤ THE POPULAR IVATT TANKS ✤
✤ NEW AND ESTABLISHED MOTIVE POWER ✤

SECTION 5:

1958 TO 1962: A HIDDEN AGENDA? ... PAGE 111

✤ BORROWED 'BLACK FIVES' ✤ BUSY BR 'FIVES' ✤ AROUND COLE ✤ MORE AROUND MIDFORD ✤
✤ BR CLASS '4' 2-6-0s AND 4-6-0s ✤ TEST RUN WITH A 'NINE' ✤ THE ARRIVAL OF THE '9F's ✤ ENTHUSIAST'S SPECIALS ✤
✤ WHIT SUNDAY EXCURSION ✤ A BUSY DAY FOR No. 92204 ✤ AROUND TEMPLECOMBE No. 2 JUNCTION ✤
✤ WINCANTON DEPARTURE ✤ SUMMER 1961: THE END OF A LONG TRADITION ✤ ROCK CUTTING BRIDGE ✤
✤ EVERCREECH JUNCTION ✤ S&D CLASS '7F' 2-8-0s STILL HARD AT WORK ✤ MODIFIED BULLIEDS ✤
✤ 1962: VARIETY STILL THE WATCHWORD ✤ NEAR SHEPTON MONTAGUE ✤ AN EXCITING FINALÉ ✤

SECTION 6:

1963 TO 1966: RUNDOWN AND CLOSURE ... PAGE 167

✤ THE CHANGING FACE OF FREIGHT TRAFFIC ✤ BRANCH LINE PASSENGER TRAFFIC ✤ MAIN LINE LOCAL TRAFFIC ✤
✤ TWO 'NINES' RETURN – ANOTHER CYNICAL PLOY? ✤ EXCURSIONS AND SPECIALS ✤ BOURNEMOUTH WEST ✤
✤ ENTHUSIASTS SPECIALS ✤ WHIT SUNDAY AT CHILCOMPTON TUNNEL ✤ FINAL FORMS OF MOTIVE POWER ✤
✤ THE 'FIRST' FINAL WEEKEND ✤ THE FINAL FINALÉ ✤ THE LAST TWO SPECIALS ✤

Norman Lockett enjoys a visit to the footplate of BR Standard Class '5' 4-6-0, No. 73047, courtesy of well known senior S&D driver, Donald Beale. The photograph is not attributed but, possibly, was taken by Norman's good friend, Ivo Peters.

FRONT COVER PICTURE: **Yet to receive its BR number and still carrying the legend 'LMS' on the tender, S&D class '7F' 2-8-0 No. 13805 emerges from Combe Down Tunnel and heads down the gradient towards Midford with the 3.45pm Bath to Evercreech Junction freight.** *20th April 1949*

REAR COVER PICTURE: **Johnson Class '1P' 0-4-4T No. 58047 approaches Church Street level crossing in Highbridge town with the 2.35pm Burnham to Highbridge train. The signal box controlled the single line to Burnham-on-Sea and the parallel set of rails on the left, which gave access to the sidings at the Wharf.** *6th October 1950*

FOREWORD

Like most aspects of modern day life, the 'noble art' of railway photography bears little resemblance today to that of fifty or more years ago. I make this as an introductory comment because I recall when – now more than twenty years ago – I first looked through what must have been only a fraction of the many black & white prints created by Norman Lockett, I was rather surprised by just how often the same locations appeared to be featured. What, of course, I had forgotten was the fact that, in pursuit of his hobby, Norman operated under constraints and using equipment a world away from that which, nowadays, we take for granted.

As to those constraints; well, for starters, Norman relied entirely on public transport. Not for him, nor for most of his contemporaries, the convenience enjoyed by today's photographers, who can jump into the car and drive to some convenient spot close to a favourite line-side location, perhaps as far removed from home as a hundred miles or more. Then, of course, there were the constraints imposed by the fact that, as with most employees, Norman was required – certainly until the early 1960s – to work a 5½ day week, with each full day (including travelling time to and from work) accounting for nearly 12 hours.

Following eight years of training, Norman Lockett was registered as a druggist and, in 1934, became a member of the Pharmaceutical Society. His entire career was in the employ of Boots the Chemist, with many years spent as the manager of various West Country branches. As such, on Thursdays & Saturdays, Norman worked an extra 'rota-hour' from 6pm to 7pm, in order to dispense medical prescriptions. All of this resulted in most of his pictures being taken, of necessity, on Wednesday afternoons and Sundays. Even Bank Holiday visits to a more distant line-side location were only possible if Norman did not have to open the shop for rota-duty early in the evening!

Holiday leave provided the only real opportunity to plan for photography well away from the home town and being in the 'service sector', one week's leave usually had to be taken outside the traditional high summer holiday period.

So, all of these factors are reflected in Norman's photographic collection which dates from April 1934 until 1983. Many of his pre-war photographs were taken around Plymouth, at such locations as Hemerdon Incline and Cornwood. Norman's years spent working in Bristol, whilst living in Weston-super-Mare (his home town), ensured that many lineside locations local to both of these places featured very prominently from the early post-war era. It should come as no surprise, therefore, that – first and foremost – Norman was very much a fan of all things Great Western! Later on, whilst living and working in Bath, the Somerset & Dorset line was visited far more frequently (although, as we will see in this album, the S&D, including around Highbridge and Burnham, was no stranger to Norman in earlier days). During this post-1958 period, Norman's friendship with Ivo Peters undoubtedly influenced some of the locations visited.

Norman's photographic excursions involved quite a heavy load; two cameras including a large, quarter plate size, Thornton-Pickard Reflex model using glass plate negatives; two cases each holding a dozen slide-holders loaded with unexposed glass plates; together with notebooks and timetables. All very different to the convenience of today's digital cameras! One consequence of this will be noted in the captions to some of the photographs in this book. Because Norman's camera was so bulky, he was not always able to put it

down in time to record the number of the second locomotive on a double-header. Likewise, it was not the best of equipment with which to struggle to the lineside through deep snow; so you will see no photographs of the S&D during the arctic winter of 1962/63.

The large majority of the photography was carried out between the months of April and October. Development of the glass plate negatives would be undertaken, by Norman, late at night, usually within a week or so of the photographs having been taken. Printing, enlarging and mounting would await the 'closed' season – November to March. Norman's professional training was to serve him well in both the development and printing of his photographs, as witnessed by the superb quality of his prints.

Undoubtedly, Norman's style was heavily influenced by many of his contemporaries dating from the pre-Second World War era. He was, as I believe it is sometimes called, an exponent of the 'three-quarter front view', although, as will be seen in the following pages, he was far from averse from including much of the background detail and especially the scenery in his photographs. As a member of the Railway Photographic Society, he would make mounted enlargements of some of what he considered to be the best of each year's photographs. Other members of the Society would do likewise and these folios would be circulated amongst members for comment.

Norman Lockett had his favourite locations for photography, within the constraints to which we referred earlier. Even so, over the passage of thirty years he managed to visit much of the line. Because of this, however, the book does not cover every location on the S&D, although there are one or two places which were rarely photographed by anyone else which appear here, whilst Norman also managed to find a few quite different viewpoints at some of the locations. In order to get the best out of the pictures, bearing in mind the size of the glass plate negatives, many are printed full page, so the reader is in for a fair amount of book turning, for which we apologise. A number have also been presented double-page, to allow readers to lose themselves in the beautiful locations featured. We recognise that some purists will be offended but, for this we do not apologise! Ultimately, if more than 200 superb quality photographs of the Somerset & Dorset (of which only about twenty have previously been published) are your *forté*, then we trust you will be pleased by what appears on the following pages.

David and I would not be so bold (or naive!) to suggest this is the last single major collection of photographs featuring the S&D line to have remained unpublished. Even all these years after the sad demise of the famous old line, it never ceases to amaze me what still comes out of the woodwork. That said, however, there cannot be too many as yet unpublished collections to match the quality and quantity achieved by Norman Lockett. Of all the photographers associated with the Somerset & Dorset line in the 1950s and early 1960s, the name Ivo Peters immediately comes to mind. Ivo and Norman became great friends and, in the final decade of the steam era, often travelled the country together photographing the railway scene. Years later, I recall asking Ivo whom he considered amongst the finest of his contemporaries. Without a moment's hesitation, Ivo responded *"In terms of quality that has to be my old friend, Norman Lockett."* From Ivo, to whom quality meant everything, that was praise indeed!

Mike Arlett

INTRODUCTION

So why *The Somerset & Dorset 1935-1966*, when 1936-1966 has a much better symmetry for a sub-title? Well, it just happens, Norman Lockett took his first two photographs of the S&D in 1935 – simple as that! You see, this book is **not** intended to be another detailed illustrated history of the Somerset & Dorset Railway. It is a record of one man's visits to the line – or to be more accurate, some parts of the line – over a period from 1935 to 1966, excluding the years of the Second World War during which Norman Lockett took no railway photographs. It also includes some of the many facts and personal memories about the S&D which Norman's photographs have prompted Mike to recall. So, if you have reached this far without thinking "*Oh, not another book of the S&D*", then we are reasonably confident you must be an enthusiast of (or at least mildly interested in) the Somerset & Dorset line as it existed during the final thirty years prior to the withdrawal of all passenger services and closure of all but a few miles of track in March 1966. If so, we trust this book will not disappoint.

Norman Lockett's approach to his photography and the fact that (for the reasons already explained in the foreword) he did not or was unable to visit many of the locations on the line, have made it necessary for us to take a different approach to setting out the content of this book. We have explored, in turn, the various passages of time during the thirty year period, as portrayed by Norman's visits to the lineside. Each of these chosen periods of time forms the subject of a chapter in this book, within which we have elected to adopt a series of unrelated 'themes'. We hope, in taking this approach, to have succeeded in conveying some of the atmosphere of this lovely old line. In any case, we did not wish this book to be another which portrayed the railway in geographical order; that is a visual trip from one end of the main line (and the branch line) to the other. Even so, we think it appropriate to include a map of the line, not least because there are a small number of locations featured in the following pages with which some readers may be less familiar.

Again, reflecting the constraints imposed on Norman Lockett's time at the lineside, we must own up now to this book (like several before) having a distinct bias towards various locations along the northern section of the line between Bath and Evercreech Junction. However, at least our justification for this is unlike the reason more usually given – '*because it covers the most interesting section of the line*'. In any case, the content of this book, we hope, differs from much of what has gone before insofar that it features mostly previously unpublished photographs, including the years leading up to and immediately following the Second World War. Emphasis has been given to the study of locomotive types; combinations of motive power; specific lineside locations – many well known, some not so; and the variety of traffic. In fact, most of those facets of the line which has made the Somerset & Dorset so very special to that large army of people interested in railway and industrial heritage.

We have given some prominence to pictures taken by Norman prior to the start of the 1960s, with particular emphasis on the post-war years of the 1940s and into the early 1950s. So whilst the overall number of different locations included might appear limited compared with later years, we have endeavoured to cover with greater emphasis a period seldom featured in such detail in many of the previous publications which, more often, have been slanted more towards the final sad years of the S&D. That is not to say we have overlooked the last years of the existence of the line but we also wanted to ensure that

we included a good selection of motive power from a period before the use of the BR 'Standards' became ever more prevalent.

We are not overly concerned that the photographs we have included from the last few years of the S&D might be similar to some of those taken, for example, by Norman's great friend Ivo Peters, not least because, despite the fact that they may have photographed the same train at the same location, they often took up quite different lineside positions in order to obtain their respective photographs. As is very evident from the pages of this book, Norman did not overlook the 'train in the countryside' approach to photography. It is, however, a fact that he commenced his hobby in an era when portrait photographs of locomotives and trains (invariably 'three-quarters front') was the accepted style, even if this sometimes meant him heavily cropping the area printed to remove some background included on the negative. Needless to say, such background is nowadays of considerably greater interest, so, wherever appropriate, we have ensured the full size of the original plate has been reproduced within the pages of this book. Others may know with more certainty but David believes that these often tightly cropped portrait style shots were very much the required format for submitting photographs to the Railway Photographic Society during the 1950s and for his father to have done otherwise might well have invoked some adverse comment. This would certainly accord with something Ivo Peters once told Mike, that, many years ago, when he first submitted for exhibition some of his 'railway in the landscape' photographs, he came under a certain amount of mild derision from some 'traditionalists'!

Norman Lockett took his hobby very seriously and the quality of the finished print was as important (perhaps more important) than taking a chance, attempting a shot which might prejudice the opportunity to achieve the best possible result with the finished print. This dedication to quality was obviously one reason why Norman continued to use a large-format press camera and glass plate negatives, long after many other serious railway photographers had transferred their allegiance to smaller (and more convenient) formats. It's a little like the situation existing at the start of the 21st century, where there has been a reluctance by some serious photographers to abandon film and move to the use of a digital camera!

Very few of Norman Lockett's railway photographs of the S&D have been previously published. Some could be seen, just occasionally during the 1950s, in periodicals such as *Trains Illustrated*; a handful have been provided for use by other authors, whilst some have appeared in specialist publications, such as the S&DR Trust's calendar or house magazine, mostly now many years ago. We are confident, therefore, that all but an insignificant number of the pictures reproduced herein have never before appeared in the public domain.

Because the quality of the finished print meant so much to Norman, obviously we have wished to ensure that reproduction in this book will meet what were his own demanding standards. To this end, we are delighted to have 'teamed up' with Lightmoor Press, in the knowledge that if precedence – as evidenced by earlier publications – is anything to go by, our publisher will not compromise on quality issues. We also wished to ensure a reasonable number of the prints were reproduced to a large format; again in the knowledge that this is how Norman would have wished his work to be portrayed. So, we are extremely grateful to our publishing team, and in particular to Neil Parkhouse, not only for ensuring we can achieve our aims but for all the helpful advice and encouragement he has given.

David has spent very many hours working his way through every one of the thousands of glass plate negatives and, with the benefit of a top-of-the-range scanner, has produced a digital image from just about every negative within the collection which features the S&D. These he emailed to Mike so that a decision could be made as to what to include in our book. The selected plates were then rescanned at a high resolution by our publisher, whilst Mike continued the tasks of research, writing and captioning. The final scans included not only all of those negatives never, apparently, printed out but all bar three of the negatives for which a print had been made, previously, by Norman. The exceptions are the result of David being unable to 'track down' the glass plates, so our publisher has been forced to make scans from the prints (for your information, these are the pictures on pages 132, 149 and 154/5). The reason for returning to the plates where possible was that we were surprised to find how much 'information' had been lost in the making of what looked to be nice 'contrasty' prints (which was the way most railway photographers from Norman's era appeared to prefer it!), such as sky effects, smoke and locomotive detail otherwise in shadow. Such are the advantages of the 'digital era' that we have been able to undertake and coordinate our respective tasks with relative ease, despite David, Mike and our publisher all living many miles apart.

It has proved very interesting to view each new scan in the realisation that, in many instances, this is probably the first time the negative has ever been 'printed', the earliest glass plates now being more than seventy years old. We make this assumption on the strength of David being unable to find any evidence that Norman had ever made a print. Bearing in mind the total number of negatives in the entire collection, this is not surprising; we suspect Norman never had sufficient time to make a print of every photograph he took! No doubt, as he viewed each latest batch of glass plates, he selected, there and then, those which he would print during the following winter months. Because we have included so many previously unprinted shots, we hope this will add greatly to the interest of this book, especially where we have identified a location or, for example, a particular lineside structure which has never or only rarely featured in previous publications about the Somerset & Dorset.

Despite careful storage, some of the glass plates have deteriorated; a few to the extent that, had it not been for the improvements and 'repairs' which can be achieved with digital imaging and photo-editing software, several of the pictures included in the following pages would have been unusable. There were also periods when it appears Norman was unable to source his preferred choice of glass plate negatives. This left him with no option other than the temporary use of alternative plates and, in some cases, film stock, neither of which have survived the passage of time quite so well. Whilst we have limited the inclusion of these, a few have been used where the subject matter was of sufficient interest to outweigh any shortcomings in the quality of the negative.

In preparing the notes and captions, Mike has deliberately kept to a minimum any cross-referencing between various pictures. The 'down side' of this is the need to sometimes replicate various details and data. Still, it's better than the alternative of constant page turning, backwards and forth, in order to track down where such information might otherwise be found! Mike wishes to apologise in advance for the number of times he might have (has!) mentioned that by far the most picturesque part of the line lay in the vicinity of Midford (but he is, unashamedly, totally biased on this point – and possibly correct!)

We wish to thank our wives, Daphne and Sandra for their support over the twenty-four months during which much of our spare time has been sacrificed in pursuit of this book, often to the detriment of other 'duties'. Both wives are not, to date, aware that this volume will, we hope, form the first of a number of such illustrated books featuring the Norman Lockett Archive which we have in mind. Only time, their continued forbearance, our stamina, and the good will of our publisher will determine whether we actually achieve this objective. Our other acknowledgements are recorded separately below.

David Lockett & Mike Arlett 2008

ACKNOWLEDGEMENTS

In addition to his own knowledge and memories of the Somerset & Dorset, Mike has made use of various publications and journals in researching details for this book. Of these, the most prominent has been the *Pines Express*, the Bulletin of the Somerset & Dorset Railway Trust, the activities of which, over the past forty years, have done so much to keep alive the memories of the old S&D. Our thanks, in particular, to Dr Peter Cattermole, the Trust's former Chairman and, more recently, former Archivist, for arranging repeated access to the impressive museum and archive housed at Washford station on the West Somerset Railway. Running the S&DRT a close second has been the *Railway Observer*, the house magazine of the Railway Correspondence & Travel Society, which provides such a wonderful source of motive power and associated information. Mike has also drawn freely from the *Railway Magazine*, *Trains Illustrated* and many of the books and articles which have been written about the S&D.

Special thanks are extended to Richard Strange who, for as long as can be recalled, has never failed to respond to Mike's queries – usually regarding the history of the allocations of a specific locomotive; indeed, it is a source of wonderment that Richard can come forward, by return, with so much detailed information – sometimes disproving facts that have previously appeared in print! Thanks also to Julian Jefferson, an 'IT wizard' who is the webmaster for the Somerset & Dorset Railway Heritage Trust, based at the former S&D station at Midsomer Norton, and who provided the map for this book.

Another source plundered at will has been the superb series of books entitled *Midland Railway Locomotives* published by Irwell Press. This and a similar series still lack (to date) a title dealing specifically with a fully illustrated review of Somerset & Dorset locomotives. However, we have been able to turn to and wish to acknowledge our use of *Somerset & Dorset Locomotive History* by Bradley & Milton, published in 1973 by David & Charles, a title now long out of print.

Finally, our thanks to any who, inadvertently, we may have forgotten to mention specifically. In having such a wealth of information available, Mike has endeavoured to add at least some new information whilst, hopefully, not adding too significantly to the erroneous information which has sometimes found its way into print!

The calm of a sunny early winter Sunday morning at Midford is shattered by the eruption of steam from the safety valves of S&D Class '7F' 2-8-0 No. 53802, in charge of an engineer's train. Once the summer running season had ended on the S&D, Sunday was always the obvious choice for permanent way and other engineering works for the simple reason that no public services ran, thus giving the permanent way teams uninterrupted access. Normally, Midford Signal Box would have remained closed from the very early hours of Sunday morning, after the last of the Saturday night Up freights from Evercreech Junction had cleared the Midford-Bath Junction single line section, until around 2.30am on the Monday morning, in time to receive the 'Down Mail'. Here, however, was the opportunity to earn some overtime on what would otherwise be a rest day. Of the three regular Midford signalmen, more often than not this task fell to Percy Savage, on account of him living just yards away, in a cottage in the shadow of the viaduct. The other two signalmen, Harry Wiltshire and Charlie Eyre, both lived at Wellow. From Norman's photograph, it is evident the Midford based p.way gang (Gang No. 180) were in attendance – as revealed by the open door of the trolley hut. Norman Lockett recorded in his diary notes that No. 53802 was *'on ballast train for removal of siding'*. This would have been in connection with the removal of the Up siding, which was situated just beyond the south end of Midford Viaduct and was controlled by Midford 'B' Ground Frame which, in turn had to be released by an interlocking lever (No. 11) in Midford Signal Box. Removal of the siding came as no surprise; what very little use was made of it in the latter years was, I suspect, for engineering or emergency purposes – I saw only one wagon in the siding during all my years of visits here.

Prominent in Norman's picture is Midford Signal Box, which comprised a partially rebuilt base and a 'temporary' superstructure of a style which set it apart from all other S&D boxes. This was the consequence of a 'runaway train' incident in 1936, which saw the original box severely damaged. The temporary replacement top lasted thirty-one years, until the box was demolished, the year following closure of the line. Norman obtained this view by standing on the parapet wall towards the northern end of the eight-arch viaduct and it is easy here to appreciate how the railway and single-platform station had been constructed on a ledge cut into the steeply sloping hillside. Also in view are the Down starting signal (soon to be replaced by a WR lower quadrant arm on a tubular post, which looked totally alien on the S&D!), the Up starter at the far end of the platform and (just visible to the right of the steam escaping from No. 53802) the arm of the Shunt from Platform to Up Line signal (shaped like an elongated 'X' and often referred to as a 'wrong road' or 'backing' signal). The house on the hillside was (or rather is – it's still there) *Hazel Elm*, the home of the stationmaster who, at that time, was Bob Ryan. *8th November 1959*
I had better stop as I could go on boring you 'ad infinitum' about the S&D at Midford. In any case, this picture was selected primarily for my wife, Sandra, who – when my fiancée – sometimes accompanied me on evening visits to the box during the early 1960s.

OPPOSITE PAGE: **Just across the viaduct from the picture above and some fourteen months earlier, the 10.28am (SO) Manchester (London Road)-Bournemouth West, hauled by SR 'West Country' Pacific No. 34099** *Lynmouth* **and piloted by LMR Class '4F' 0-6-0 No. 44417, leaves the single line section which extended nearly four miles from Bath Junction. Both locomotives will have been drifting through Midford station (where the single line tablet will have been given up) in order to observe the 35mph speed limit imposed over the facing points and both will now be opened up to attack the 1 in 60 gradient which carried the line around the reverse curves towards Wellow.** *13th September 1958*

THE HISTORICAL BIT

Should there still remain anybody with even the most casual interest in the railways of the British Isles who has yet to learn of the history of the Somerset & Dorset Railway, we refer you to the book of that same title as written by Robin Atthill. Originally published by David & Charles in 1967 (and since reprinted on several occasions), it was the first book on the line to appear after closure of the S&D in March 1966. As a general history it remains unsurpassed although, over the following decades, many other books – both pictorial or dealing with more specific aspects of the S&D – have, and will no doubt continue to appear, such is *still* the fascination of this unique cross-country line.

The Somerset & Dorset Railway was created in 1862 by the amalgamation of the Somerset Central Railway and the Dorset Central Railway. Always wanting for sufficient capital and adequate income, in 1874 it completed a bold and costly venture to extend its Burnham to Wimborne line from Evercreech, across the Mendip Hills, to link up with the Midland Railway at Bath. This created a through route from the North of England (and via the L&SWR at Wimborne, later at Broadstone) to Poole and Bournemouth on the south coast but it exhausted the perilous finances and other resources of the Company. Salvation was achieved via a 999 year lease to the Midland and London & South Western railway companies in 1875. Thus was created the Somerset & Dorset Joint Railway. The Grouping of the railways in 1923, to create the 'Big Four', saw the former lessees – now the London Midland & Scottish and Southern railway companies – take over ownership of the line. It was during the following thirty years that the railway was considerably improved, including doubling much (but by no means all) of the main line. In 1930, the separate management of the S&DJR came to an end and with it, the closure of the locomotive works at Highbridge and the disappearance of the distinctive Prussian Blue livery carried by the Somerset & Dorset's passenger locomotives and coaching stock.

It was just a few years later, during the mid-1930s, that Norman Lockett first started to photograph the S&D line and this brief overview of the history of the line during the thirty years which followed, until closure in 1966, will be taken forward, stage by stage, as the start of each section in this book.

'Bulldog' 0-6-0 Class '3F' No. 3211 eases a freight train through the S&D station at Highbridge. Immediately beyond the footbridge, the S&D line crossed the GW Bristol-Taunton main line on the level to reach the S&D goods shed, the Wharf and the single line to Burnham. Part of the original Somerset Central Railway station building, dating from 1854, can just be seen behind No. 3211. The far end of the platform from which Norman took this photograph was linked to the GWR station. This was set at an angle to the larger S&D station. It's rather appropriate that this, the first of Norman Lockett's S&D photographs, should feature a locomotive supplied new to the S&DJR. As No. 66, she had arrived from Derby early in 1896, the last of an order placed by the Joint Committee for five of these Johnson 0-6-0s. When photographed here, the locomotive had already been in service for thirty-nine years, during which time she had been twice re-boilered. On being taken into LM&S stock in 1930, No. 66 was allocated the number as seen above. Renumbered again by BR in 1948 (as 43211), although no longer allocated to the S&D line, this old workhorse was destined to remain in service until mid-1961. *April 1935*

The platform from which Norman obtained his photograph was – at that time – less than three years old, the S&D Joint Committee having agreed the original structure be renewed. The replacement, formed of precast concrete units and erected towards the end of 1932, appears to have been provided from the SR concrete works at Exmouth Junction. The footbridge was also a replacement, no doubt coming from the same source. The platform seat and gas lamp are of older lineage and would both be considered as 'collector's items' today!

Section 1

The 1930s

A First Visit to the S&D

Norman Lockett appears to have first visited the S&D, at Highbridge, in April 1935, at which time he was living in Plymouth. Perhaps it was during a journey to or from his home town of Weston-super-Mare that he happened to make a mental note of this 'other' railway which, unusually, crossed his route on the level. Ironically, although a dedicated GWR enthusiast, he never photographed the main line to the West of England at Highbridge station, so what brought him to the S&D station we will never know.

In the 1930s, the small town of Highbridge must have been a fairly depressed place. In 1923, the S&DJR – leased to the Midland Railway and the L&SWR since 1875 – had passed into the ownership of the successors of those lessees, the London, Midland & Scottish and the Southern railway companies. This, of course, was a consequence of the Railways Act of 1921, which consolidated 123 separate railway companies into the 'Big Four', a process known as 'the Grouping'. The new owners invested in some additional motive power for the S&D and, faced with growing competition from road transport, opened five new halts but economic reforms were essential and, from 1st July 1930, the separate management of the S&D was

abandoned. The motive power had already been absorbed into the LM&S at the start of the year and now the coaching stock was divided between the two owning companies. The famous Prussian Blue livery of the S&D soon passed into memory.

At Highbridge, the locomotive and carriage works were run down and, in May 1930, closed with the loss of around 300 jobs. In 1933, the shipping interests of the S&D, which were centred on Highbridge Wharf, were abandoned, although some other seaborne traffic continued to make decreasing use of the wharf for a further fifteen years, a Dutch coaster, discharging a load of timber in June 1948, being probably the last cargo of significance to be received. British Railways officially closed the wharf to shipping the following year.

Having taken just the two photographs reproduced here, Norman Lockett appears not to have revisited the S&D in the Highbridge area until the start of the 1950s. However, something must have stirred his interest, because he did make some lineside forays to the S&D main line, although it has to be admitted, because he was still living in Plymouth, these visits to the S&D were not at all regular.

Johnson Class '1P' 0-4-4T No. 1350 waits at Highbridge with a branch line service from Burnham. The S&DJR had purchased the first of what became a total of fourteen 0-4-4Ts in 1877 but, by 1932, all except one had been scrapped. However, the LM&S provided replacements from its own stock of the same MR design, No. 1350 being one such example. Built at Derby in 1892 and originally entering service as No. 1697, the stay at Highbridge (with an intermediate transfer to and from Bristol Barrow Road) lasted only a few years. Reported as seen working on the Glastonbury-Wells branch in 1941, the locomotive was transferred from Highbridge to Burton in February 1942. Passing into BR stock in 1948 and renumbered 58058, this 0-4-4T survived until condemned and cut up in October 1952, after a planned intermediate repair at Derby had been reassessed. *April 1935*

Norman recorded this train as a Bradford to Bournemouth express hauled by Class '2P' 4-4-0 No. 634 and a Class '4F' 0-6-0. Notice how the two tracks start to diverge as they approach the bridge on which Norman was standing to take this picture, S&D Bridge No. 28 near Stoney Littleton just south-west of Wellow. This is an indication that, when this section of the S&D was doubled in 1894, Stoney Littleton Bridge (its official name) was widened by the provision of a second arch built alongside the original single-line structure, which dated from 1874. This was the first overbridge south of Bath to be widened by this method, which was adopted at many other locations down the line. *14th August 1936*

All of the bridges on the S&D were numbered, those on the main line starting from 'Bridge No. 1' near Bath Junction, where the S&D joined the Midland Railway, and finishing in the south at the junction at Wimborne, the original junction with the former L&SWR. After the construction of the cut-off line between Corfe Mullen and Broadstone, the S&D bridge numbering was continued via that route, taking the next available numbers following those used towards Wimborne. The S&D maintained an official record ('Bridge List') of all numbered bridges and tunnels, including details of the type of construction. Thus 'Stoney Littleton Bridge' (No. 28) comprised: 'Down Side, Masonry Arch on Masonry Abutments. Up Side, Brick Arch on Masonry Abutments, and Pier Arch and Pier faced with Blue Bricks.' Note the differing materials used in the existing (1874) single line bridge and the later (1894) second arch, built when the line was doubled.

1930S MOTIVE POWER

To those of you who, like the writer, first came to know the S&D line in the 1950s and who enthuse about the wonderful diversity of motive power to be seen during that era, it should be stated this bore little resemblance to just twenty years earlier, when the variety of locomotives operating on the main line was rather more limited. Generally, throughout most of the 1930s, the more important through passenger and semi-fast trains were hauled by the Class '2P' 4-4-0s; the local stopping trains might still bring forth an elderly 0-4-4T; the '4F' 0-6-0s were used on both passenger and freight traffic, whilst the S&D '7F' 2-8-0s handled the heavy mineral and freight trains. On summer Saturdays, the through holiday traffic was becoming ever busier and such trains crossed the Mendips behind a brace of 4-4-0s or 0-6-0s, or a combination of both. Less frequently, the 0-6-0 might be a Class '3F'. All were of ex-Midland or London, Midland & Scottish designs, some having been built for the S&DJR, but that was about as much variety as the lineside observer might witness! True, there were just a few more at specific locations, such as the pair of Sentinel 4-wheeled shunters, purchased

for the S&D in 1929 for use at Radstock, together with a number of LM&S Standard Class '3' 0-6-0 tank engines. These, however, were replacements for some of the earlier locomotives and at the start of the 1930s, the forward-looking LM&SR took little time in withdrawing from service much of the elderly stock it had inherited from the S&D system.

The policy of replacing time-worn locomotives with less elderly stock of much the same design lasted until 1938. Three years earlier the LM&S undertook a review of motive power requirements for the S&D and following some trials, a number of Stanier Class '5' 4-6-0s were allocated to the line. This had been made possible by a bridge rebuilding and strengthening programme on the Midland line from Mangotsfield to Bath, following which the Stanier '5's were permitted to use that route. So at last, in 1938, there was something new to photograph. However, in early September of the following year, the outbreak of the Second World War immediately put an end to the photographic pursuits of Norman Lockett and he would not recommence his hobby until 1946.

It's 12 noon as a pair of Class '2P' 4-4-0s, Nos. 632 (leading) and 629, head north-eastwards from Wellow with the Up 'Pines Express'. The rear of the train is passing over Wellow Viaduct (No. 22), whilst Norman had positioned himself on the side of the cutting adjacent to the overbridge officially named 'Morris's Bridge' (No. 21). This was another short section of the line where those who planned the route of the 'Bath Extension' had found it necessary to take a much more direct line than the former 'Radstock arm' of the Somersetshire Coal Canal and the tramway which superseded this length of the waterway. Hereabouts, these had followed the natural contours by means of a 180 degree loop around the north slope of the hillside. In later years, this view of the railway became a favourite of many photographers from which to record S&D traffic. *14th August 1936*
Notice, nestling amongst the trees, the tower of St Julian's Church, where the bells had rung out in celebration to welcome the very first train along this section of the line early in the morning of 20th July 1874.

Photographed between 1936 and 1938 (unusually, the date was unrecorded), 0-4-4T Class '1P' No. 1408 drifts down the 1 in 60 gradient past Midford Up Siding, a facility which – even at this time – was little used. Note the very tall Down advanced starting signal in the background, which remained a feature here until replaced at the start of the 1960s. No. 1408 was one of a batch of ten of the 0-4-4Ts ordered by the Midland Railway in 1898 and built by Dübs & Co. The locomotive originally entered service as No. 781 and was withdrawn in 1947. L&SWR 3-coach set No. 417 looks to have been recently repainted; it lasted in service until 1949. Notice how the track had been laid on a cant. The maintenance of this twisting section of the railway was, like the S&D line in general, always to a high standard, so different from the very earliest days of the Company, when the cash-strapped Somerset & Dorset Railway was not renowned for the state of its permanent way!

Another of the classic S&D locations is featured here, as S&D Class '7F' 2-8-0 No. 13804, with a Bath to Evercreech freight, approaches 'Bridge 69', situated about 80 yards before the summit of the line was reached at Masbury. This heavy train has been assisted at the rear for the 7½ mile climb from Radstock by a Class '3F' 0-6-0T. *8th June 1938*

The 'banker' ran coupled to the guard's van from Radstock until passing the Down home signal at Binegar. Here, the guard used a special uncoupling hook (a close-up view is included on page 169) to lift the three-link coupling, the banker then continuing to assist uncoupled until just before the rear part of the freight reached the end of the climb. Then, having drawn to a halt and seen the guard's van pass safely over the summit, the crew would return their locomotive to Binegar, running 'wrong line'. This latter movement was protected by a special banking staff, which had been collected from the lineside mechanical exchange apparatus a few minutes earlier whilst passing Binegar on the southbound journey. Had the guard been unable to uncouple the banker whilst passing the signal at Binegar, the train would be halted to perform the operation from the ground, two minutes being added to the running time to allow for the stop. The fun really started when the assisting engine failed to collect the bank engine staff, perhaps as a result of the pouch holding the staff being knocked to the ground. The instructions required the train to be halted. Whatever the potential problem – such as single line working or non-release of the banking staff – there were printed instructions in the Sectional Appendix to the Working Time Tables to cover such contingencies.

When the loading of a passenger train exceeded 190 tons (the equivalent of a maximum of six coaches) between Bath and Evercreech Junction, invariably the Class '2P' 4-4-0 usually allocated would be substituted by a Class '4F' 0-6-0. However, when the loading exceeded 230 tons, double-heading was necessary. This might be a pair of 4-4-0s or 0-6-0s or, as here, a combination of both types with '4F' No. 4046 attached ahead of '2P' No. 629 in charge of the Down 'Pines Express', heading south-west of Wellow, towards Shoscombe. The overgrown condition of the hedgerow (as also seen earlier at this same location) bordering so close to the Up side of the line was unusual by S&D standards. *14th August 1936*

Having just emerged from Combe Down Tunnel, a pair of Class '2P' 4-4-0s, No's 697 (leading) and 700, cross Tucking Mill Viaduct heading towards Midford with a Bournemouth express. These two locomotives had only recently been allocated to the S&D line; No. 697 to Bath by mid-1935 and No. 700 to Templecombe in June 1936. Both were LM&S-built examples of the final development of the former Midland Railway 4-4-0s, No. 700 being the very last of the class to be constructed, entering service in 1932. The tall wooden-posted Midford Down distant signal seen here was to be replaced by a new post fifteen feet high and with an upper quadrant arm on 22nd March 1942. This viewpoint shows well how this viaduct had been widened in 1894, in anticipation of the laying of a second set of rails, a project which, as explained later, never materialised. Incidentally, the house seen on the hillside, top left, situated in Summer Lane, Combe Down, must have enjoyed a wonderful view of the line across Tucking Mill Viaduct. *14th August 1936*

THE S&D CLASS '7F' 2-8-0S (1914 SERIES)

Arguably, no other class of locomotive has come to personify the Somerset & Dorset more than the '7F' 2-8-0s, no doubt because two out of the total of just eleven which were constructed especially for the S&DJR, can still be seen today, at work on heritage lines.

On these two pages are representatives of the original batch of six locomotives (S&D No's 80-85) built by the Midland Railway at Derby and delivered in 1914. A further five (No's 86-90) were constructed by Robert Stephenson & Co. Ltd and delivered in 1925. These (examples of which will be seen later on) had a larger boiler of 5ft 3ins diameter, compared with 4ft 7⅞ins for the earlier series. The two series also differed in that the first were right-hand drive whilst those of 1925 lineage were driven from the left side. Their subsequent history has been well documented; suffice to say here that, when absorbed into LM&S stock in 1930, they were at first renumbered 9670-80 but just two years later renumbered as 13800-10. It was during this period when Norman Lockett first photographed these impressive machines. Over a period from 1930 to 1955, the later series all received the smaller size boiler carried by the earlier locomotives in this class.

SOUTHERN AND LONDON MIDLAND AND SCOTTISH RAILWAY COMPANIES'

SOMERSET & DORSET RAILWAY

JOINT COMMITTEE.

APPENDIX

TO THE

WORKING TIME TABLES.

FOR THE INFORMATION OF THE COMMITTEE'S SERVANTS ONLY.

1st JANUARY, 1933. UNTIL FURTHER NOTICE.

BY ORDER.

No. 13800, the doyen of the S&D Class '7F' 2-8-0s, crosses Watery Bottom Viaduct (No. 12) on the 1 in 50 climb through Lyncombe Vale, Bath, with a service which Norman recorded as the 11.10am Bath-Shepton Mallet goods, although I suspect it is likely that this freight in fact ran through to Evercreech Junction. The local gangers have yet to cut down the summer growth along this section of the lineside. Notice also the profusion of glasshouses high up on the hillside, located to take full advantage of the southern slope of the valley between Devonshire and Combe Down tunnels. A nursery had existed here since before the S&D line had opened in 1874 but, as will be seen in later photographs when Norman returned here, the glasshouses were destined to be demolished, to permit the construction of some imposing semi-detached houses fronting Greenway Lane. *14th August 1936*

There were many places on the S&D where the gradient was constantly changing. A lengthy loose-coupled freight might extend across three or more different gradients at the same time! Little wonder that the S&D Appendix to the Working Time Tables (LEFT) *contained a number of instructions to drivers and guards regarding the braking of such traffic.*

Other than a brief respite at Shepton Mallet, No. 13804 had been climbing for some five miles by the time she reached this point, heading for Bath with a northbound freight from Evercreech Junction. The fireman had obviously spotted Norman from afar and called his driver across the footplate, as both men can be seen. As an aside, we pondered as to how Norman – relying only on public transport – had reached the lineside hereabouts? We think it must have been by bus from Bristol to the outskirts of Shepton Mallet, involving at least two changes of service and then by walking the lanes. It required a lot of effort just to capture two or three images! Just visible in the right background is an occupation bridge (No. 80), known as Davis's Bridge. *8th June 1938*

1938 – ANCIENT & MODERN

At the start of 1938, motive power on the S&D still mirrored that which had existed at the start of the decade, when the London, Midland & Scottish Railway took over direct responsibility. Whilst many of the older locomotives which had been built for the S&D had been scrapped, the replacements supplied by the LM&S were generally of the same design as those superseded.

Thus, for example, an elderly 0-4-4T could still be seen on the main line. Change, however, was in the air, as in March 1938 a Stanier Class '5' 4-6-0 had been tested between Bath and Bournemouth. The trial was a complete success, so six of the 'Black Fives' were transferred to Bath and, from 2nd May 1938, these commenced to work regularly over the line.

At the same location as the previous picture – little more than a mile north of Shepton Mallet station – Johnson Class '1P' 0-4-4T No. 1334 (allocated to Bath) ambles up the gradient towards Winsor Hill Tunnel and Masbury, with the 2.00pm all-stations stopping train from Templecombe to Bath. No. 1334 (originally No. 1826) was one of a batch of ten of this class built at Derby in 1889, so was nearing fifty years of age when photographed here. She was withdrawn eight years later, in 1946. *8th June 1938*

Just a short distance northwards and fifteen minutes after the previous photograph, this was Norman Lockett's first view of a 'Black Five' on the S&D. Just a month after the commencement of regular use of these fine locomotives, No. 5432 speeds the Down 'Pines Express' clear of Winsor Hill Tunnel and past the hut which contained the ground frame controlling Downside Siding. This is the only photograph the author has seen of this ground frame, which was sited immediately to the north of Bridge No. 78, the girders of this underbridge being partly visible in the foreground. Opened in 1900 to serve a quarry, Downside Siding and its attendant ground frame were taken out of use on 23rd January 1940. No. 5432 had been allocated to Bath from Crewe North in April 1938 but the stay was short-lived; most of the 'Black Fives' were transferred away at one time or another during the Second World War, which commenced just fifteen months after Norman took this picture. No. 5432 was reallocated to Leeds in September 1941. This proved to be Norman's last pre-war visit to the line. *8th June 1938*

Norman's first post-war photograph of the S&D was taken on Wednesday 24th July 1946, at 4.40pm on an overcast afternoon, amongst the tranquillity of the countryside to the south-west of Wellow. Class '4F' 0-6-0 No. 3835 heads towards Radstock with the 3.15pm Gloucester-Bournemouth semi-fast (the 4.25pm from Bath). The external cleanliness of motive power was, as yet, not a priority in returning the railways to their pre-war condition. Even so, it must have been wonderful to escape from the everyday pressures following the war years, albeit for only a couple of hours during a half-day mid-week break, to obtain this and the following view. It had been eight long years since Norman had last taken a photograph featuring the S&D. Looking at the idyllic countryside hereabouts, it must have seemed a world away from the terrible conditions imposed by the war-time bombing of Bath and Bristol, yet the centre of Bath lay only five miles to the north (about seven miles by rail), whilst the southern outskirts of Bristol were little more than a dozen miles to the north-east.

No. 3835 was the pioneer superheated 'Big Goods' which, together with No. 3836, entered service in October 1911. This was six years ahead of the start of full production of this series of Class '3' (later Class '4' designated) 0-6-0s.

Section 2
Post-War 1940s
the End of the Grouping

The outbreak of the Second World War put an immediate end to Norman Lockett's interest in railway photography as, for the duration, he was directed by his employer to transfer from town to town all across the country to manage various branches of Boots the Chemist. In 1940, his wife Louise and two children, Geoffrey and David, moved from the heavily bombed city of Plymouth back to Norman's home town of Weston-super-Mare, where his two other children Norma and Philip were born. Throughout the war years, Norman was able to travel home only occasionally.

On the S&D, the outbreak of the war resulted in a drastic reduction of passenger services, as the line (for the second time in a quarter-century) assumed a major role as a strategic route for military traffic. Much of the traditional motive power was transferred away, with replacements coming from the Southern Railway, mostly in the shape of Class 'S11' and 'T9" 4-4-0s, and Class 'T1' 0-4-4Ts.

Thankfully, the infrastructure of the S&D system escaped largely unharmed from the ravages of enemy air raids. Templecombe (SR) station suffered bomb damage whilst, overall, the former Midland and S&D running lines in and around Bath escaped relatively unscathed, having regard to the intensity of the infamous 'Baedeker' air raids and the proximity of the gas works, a prime target which, along with the Midland goods shed, received direct hits.

Norman's only other photograph during that first post-war visit was taken some forty minutes later, little more than a 100 yards further towards Stoney Littleton. Another, equally unkempt Class '4F', No. 3875, passes under Wellow Bridge with the 5.00pm 'all stations & halts stopper' from Bath to Templecombe. Bridge No. 26 carried the narrow lane from Wellow to Stoney Littleton across the line on a single iron span, so must have been built when the track to this section of the S&D between Radstock and Wellow was doubled in 1894. The proposals for the original single line, opened in 1874, showed the lane (and the tramway from Radstock – which had run along the route of the old Somersetshire Coal Canal as far as Twinhoe) being diverted here so, at best, a gated crossing must have sufficed until 1894.

With the cessation of hostilities in 1945, the Southern Railway motive power had been handed back and those types more traditionally associated with the S&D returned. It was evident that, such were the run-down conditions of the railways and of industry generally, restoration of services to pre-war levels would be far from immediate. It would prove a long hard slog, with freight traffic given precedence over the reinstatement of, for example, holiday trains. In any case the gallant efforts of the 'Big Four' companies were about to be overtaken by plans, announced in 1947, to bring the railways under the control and ownership of a national system. Matters were not helped on the S&D with the collapse, in February 1946, of two of the arches of the Up side viaduct at Bath Road, Shepton Mallet, necessitating single-line working until rebuilding was completed six months later. (When the original single S&D main line had been doubled, over a period of years between 1884 and 1894, the widening of each viaduct was achieved by erecting a new single line structure abutting the original. It was the newer of the structures at Bath Road which partially collapsed.) The following February, the

structure supporting the Down line at the same location was closed for four weeks whilst strengthening work was undertaken.

Meanwhile, Norman Lockett had been able to recommence his lineside photography, in a very limited manner, during the summer of 1946. In that same year, he was made manager of one of the branches of Boots in Bristol, which enabled him to rejoin his family in Weston-super-Mare. Such, however, were the general economic conditions, that life in the immediate post-war years was, for the general population, one of ongoing hardship, with severe shortages of food, fuel and just about every other necessity.

The severe winter of 1946/7 made matters even worse, the arctic conditions being followed, in parts of the country, by very serious flooding. Some foods, such as bread and potatoes which had been available during the war years, now became rationed. There was also a critical shortage of coal, so much so that many train services were curtailed and the Ministry of Transport ordered that nearly 1,200 steam locomotives should be converted to oil burning. As we shall see, the S&D was to witness the effects of this scheme.

Almost a month after the previous view, No. 3875 featured again with the 5pm Bath to Templecombe. Still the sun refused to show its face. On this occasion, Norman chose the lineside about half a mile to the east of Wellow. The train had just passed along one of the very few lengths of straight track on this section of the line as it approached (out of sight) the Wellow Down distant signal. Also hidden from view, Wellow Brook meandered towards Midford along the foot of the valley. The steep hill in the right background – Hinton Hill – carries the road towards Hinton Charterhouse, and is typical of most of the lanes and narrow roads leading to and from Wellow; one reason why, even as late as the start of the 1960s, Wellow station was to remain one of the best patronised on the northern end of the line. *21st August 1946*

No. 3875 was one of the Class '4' 'Big Goods' which, ignoring the first two pre-production examples, were built from 1917 to 1922 by the Midland Railway. This particular example of the class was turned out new from Derby Works in November 1918. The tender with the flared coal rails dates from a Johnson locomotive of earlier lineage. Subsequently renumbered 43875 by BR in late-1949, the locomotive was withdrawn in May 1956.

AUTUMN AROUND WELLOW

Having taken the picture opposite and whilst waiting at Wellow for his train, the 5.55pm departure to Bath (the first leg of the journey home to Weston-super-Mare), the 5.00pm Bath to Evercreech Junction freight, comprising mainly empties being returned southwards, passed through behind ex-S&DJR Class '7F' No. 13802. Note the very run-down appearance of the station canopy, with the supports painted in alternate bands of red and white – a war-time measure during black-out conditions. From memory, the station did not receive any attention for another seven years. When it was finally repainted, it would be in the brown and cream 'house colours' of BR (Western Region) who, by that date, had taken over commercial responsibility for this part of the line. As at Midford, there were some delightful views of the idyllic countryside to be had from the station. Wellow Signal Box, which also released a hand-operated crossing (little used except by those on foot) can just be seen on the Down side of the line above the rear of the train. *21st August 1946*

DOUBLE BRITISH SUMMER TIME

Prior to 1953, each of Norman Lockett's glass plate negatives is protected in a paper envelope on which he wrote the details of the image contained on the plate held therein. In addition to the locomotive and train details, exposure, etc., the notes also include the weather conditions and the time of the exposure. On the following page we move forward into 1947 and on the envelopes containing glass plates used during the summer months of that year, Norman had added the initials 'DBST' – Double British Summer Time. This had been a wartime provision, whereby the time had been advanced by one hour throughout the year and, in addition, during much of the year the time was advanced by a further hour (all this in place of the normal practice of advancing the clock by one hour for the duration of each summer only). So, in the summer of 1945, following the end of the war, the clocks went back an hour on 15th July, and another hour on Sunday 7th October (the end of normal Summer Time). In 1946, normal summer time prevailed. However, because the economy of the country was so bad, and hence the need to maximise daylight during working hours, DBST (sometimes referred to as BDST) was reintroduced from mid-April to 10th August 1947. Although, in more recent times it has been suggested DBST should be reintroduced, to date it has never again been implemented.

Seen from Primrose Hill (the lane which leads towards Twinhoe and Wellow), Class '4F' 0-6-0 No. 4417 and Stanier Class '5' No. 4844 have just crossed Midford Viaduct and regained double track with the 10.00am Manchester (London Road) to Bournemouth West. This must have been a bonus shot for Norman, because this train (the equivalent of the Down 'Pines Express', which would not regain its title until 1949) was running nearly an hour late and should have preceded the 3.00pm Down local from Bath which, more usually, provided a good connection off the Manchester-Bournemouth express.

We debated whether to severely crop the scan from Norman's original glass plate negative, thereby cutting out the trees on the left and omitting most of the overhead wires. However, after much discussion, we came to the conclusion that Norman deliberately used the wires to frame the train; he was too good a photographer not to realise what he was doing and, in any case, the glass plates were expensive and not to be wasted! Accordingly, the picture is printed here in full.

AN AFTERNOON AT MIDFORD
28TH MAY 1947

Reference was made in the foreword to this book as to how, some fifty years and more ago, many photographers were able to spend only limited time pursuing their interest. This was because of the constraints imposed by their working week and a reliance on public transport, both of which combined to determine how, when and to where a lineside visit could be made. The following short series of pictures illustrate this perfectly.

The 28th May 1947 was a Wednesday, Norman Lockett's half day mid-week break in a 5½ day working week. A lovely sunny afternoon provided the ideal opportunity to catch the train from Bristol across to Bath and then out to Midford. The latter short leg of the journey was either by bus or more likely by the 3.00pm stopping train from the Midland station. Norman had time to take just five photographs (only one of which, it appears, he subsequently printed) before returning home. However, these five views provide an intriguing record of southbound traffic over the line, during an afternoon in the last year before the S&D became a part of the new nationalised British Railways system, which came into effect from 1st January 1948. They are made all the more interesting because Norman recorded the time when each photograph was taken, so it is possible to determine the punctuality of the services.

Referring back to what has been mentioned just a few pages earlier, it will be appreciated that these idyllic scenes belie the fact that life in the British Isles in 1947 had yet to recover fully from the effects of the Second World War. This process had been additionally hindered, in the early months of the year, by atrocious weather conditions. One consequence of this, coupled with the ongoing struggle to get the industrial base back on a firm footing, was the re-introduction of the wartime measure of double summer time (see panel on previous page). Continuing serious fuel shortages meant that the weekday passenger services over the S&D remained rather sparse. However, the summer of 1947 turned very hot and it is recorded that over half the total population of the country took advantage of a week's 'holiday with pay'. On the S&D, the 1947 summer service, here just a month away, did see the reinstatement of at least a few of the Saturdays only through trains between the North of England, the Midlands and Bournemouth.

Norman had now walked more than a quarter-mile further southwards from the scene of his previous picture, to where the line ran around a succession of reverse curves through the picturesque Midford Valley, heading towards Wellow. The next Down train was the 3.35pm Bath to Evercreech Junction freight, which was photographed at 4.40pm, about 40 minutes behind schedule. This train, seen here in the charge of '4F' 0-6-0 No. 4523, was scheduled to call at all stations between Radstock and Evercreech Junction, the latter being reached as late as 9.00pm. Like many services over the S&D line, the origins of this freight could be traced back many decades. In the 1920s, running as the 3.50pm to Wimborne, it was provided primarily for 'Market & Road Van Traffic'. As such, the service was still referred to as 'The Market' by S&D staff in the 1950s.

Following the passage of 'The Market', and running some 20 minutes late, Class '2P' 4-4-0 No. 696 climbs the 1 in 60 gradient away from Midford with the 3.15pm Gloucester to Bournemouth service. A check of the timetables from just a few years later, into the early 1950s, reveals that this train provided a very good connection at Gloucester for passengers from as far north as Bradford, who had travelled southwards on 'The Devonian'.

The apparatus seen in the foreground on the outside of the nearest rail was, I suspect, associated with a treadle (unseen here against the inside edge of the same rail) which, when depressed, operated a 'Train waiting' buzzer in Midford Signal Box. The tall wooden post supporting the Up outer home signal and the ringed subsidiary arm (the shunt by Up outer home signal) was replaced just fourteen months after Norman took this sequence of photographs. The replacement lattice post, repositioned closer to the lineside hut, was much shorter and the arms were both upper quadrant, as will be seen in some some of Norman's later photographs.

Next, the 4.45pm Bath-Templecombe stopping train passed, again running twenty minutes behind schedule despite the surfeit of motive power. This was a case of 'ANR' (Assistance Not Required), with '2P' No. 326 doubtless coupled ahead of No. 634 to avoid a separate light engine path to Templecombe shed.
Coincidentally, both locomotives were originally in S&DJR stock and had carried the famous Prussian Blue livery. No. 326 was supplied by the Midland Railway in 1903. As S&D No. 69, she was rebuilt at Derby in 1921, although many would consider that the rebuilding, which included the provision of superheating, was so extensive as to constitute a new locomotive. In 1928, she was renumbered as S&D No. 43, and allocated No. 326 in 1930 when taken into LM&S stock. After 1936, No. 326 saw no further use on the S&D line except for the period between November 1946 and December 1948. No. 634 dated from June 1928 when supplied new by the LM&S as S&D No. 45, the number carried until taken into LM&S stock eighteen months later. Unlike No. 326, apart from the period during the Second World War, No. 634 remained on the S&D line, allocated variously between Bath and Templecombe sheds, until withdrawn from the latter in May 1962.

Finally, in this sequence, S&D Class '7F' 2-8-0 No. 13804 is seen in charge of the 5.30pm freight from Bath. This was a service scheduled to call only at Radstock (where, possibly, many of the empty coal wagons would be put off) before reaching Evercreech Junction. Here, after about an hour, during which time the train would be reformed, the service continued to Templecombe (for examination), Blandford and Poole, with a timetabled arrival at midnight. Later during 1947, the running of this service was amended to leave Bath fifteen minutes earlier.
When you look at this sequence of photographs, perhaps those who never knew the line may begin to understand some of the fascination of lineside locations such as the Midford and Wellow Valleys – the delightful north Somerset countryside and never being sure what motive power was about to appear around the bend! As we shall see, things were about to become even better, as an ever wider range of locomotives came to be allocated or see service on the line.

A 'BLACK FIVE' WITH THE 'PINES'

Stanier Class '5' No. 4830, which had been transferred to Bath the previous May, heads towards Wellow, having just passed the Up distant signal with the 9.45am Bournemouth-Manchester. Norman Lockett took the photograph twenty-one months before this service regained its pre-war title, the 'Pines Express' (although, apparently, the staff and many of the patrons continued to refer to the services as the 'Pines'), 20th August 1947

No. 4830 was just a month short of conversion to oil firing when this picture was taken. The arctic weather of the previous winter had added to the post-war woes suffered in Britain, one aspect of which was the ongoing chronic shortage of coal. The Ministry of Transport therefore ordered the railways to convert nearly 1,200 steam locomotives to oil-firing. Just ninety-three had been converted, when somebody in the Treasury pointed out that there might be insufficient foreign reserves to complete and maintain the programme! However, by that date, more than £2 million had been expended across the country on the fixed plant, including oil storage facilities at Bath shed – one of the locomotive depots chosen to be a part of what turned out to be an embarrassing and costly fiasco. No. 4830 ran as an oil burner from early September 1947 and was converted back to coal firing during June the following year, the entire scheme having been abandoned in May 1948.*

* Readers interested in learning more of this scheme will find a detailed article, 'Oil For Coal' by A.J. Mullay, in Railway Archive No. 12, published by Lightmoor Press in March 2006.

THE END OF AN ERA ...

... AND THE START OF ANOTHER

Just four months into the brave new dawn of 'British Railways' – not that you would guess as such from this scene! Class '2P' 4-4-0 No. 569 leans to the curve through the rock cutting just to the south of Midford viaduct. This was the afternoon Gloucester-Bournemouth service, as evidenced by the board carried on the leading carriage. Again, the train was noted as 'on time' but, unlike the northbound equivalent service (as portrayed in the top picture, opposite), the Down train, in 1947, provided a much slower journey time of 2hrs 50mins from Bath to Bournemouth. On the skyline, separating the countryside around Midford from the City of Bath, the southern slopes of Combe Down can be seen, beneath which the S&D single line tunnelled at some considerable depth for more than a mile. *14th April 1948*

OPPOSITE PAGE TOP: Two final scenes taken before the railways were Nationalised. Class '2P' 4-4-0 No. 698 heads away from Wellow with the 11.40am departure from Bournemouth which, by this date, had become a service to Gloucester (on Mondays to Thursdays), to Derby (Fridays only), and to Nottingham (Saturdays only). The scene is just east of Wellow village, part of which can be seen in the left background. The rear of the train had just cleared the 4-arch Wellow Viaduct. Norman Lockett recorded the time as 1.40pm, so the train was on schedule for a 'right-time' arrival at Bath at 1.52pm; an overall timing from Bournemouth which was within a couple of minutes of that allowed for the 'Pines'. *20th August 1947*
Prior to the Second World War, the 11.40am from Bournemouth had, for many years, been a through train to the North (usually shown as a Bournemouth-Bradford service but with carriages or connections to York and Lincoln).

OPPOSITE PAGE BOTTOM: Class '4F' 0-6-0 No. 4558 (originally S&D No. 58 built in 1922) passes through the cutting a half-mile west of Wellow with the 6.48am stopping train from Bournemouth, a leisurely service which included a 30 minute wait at Templecombe and was due into Bath at 11.00am. Like many of the local passenger services over the S&D, the origins of this train could be traced back very many years, a feature which – despite impending Nationalisation – would remain little changed for at least another decade. *20th August 1947*

Class '4F' 0-6-0 No. 44559 and a Stanier 4-6-0 Class '5' speed down the gradient from Winsor Hill towards Shepton Mallet, with the southbound 'Pines Express'. The leading locomotive, one of five built for the S&D by Armstrong Whitworth & Co. in 1922, had just undergone a third change of number, although by a quirk of fate, what became the last two digits never changed! The 'Armstrong' (as each of these loco's was known on the S&D) entered service as S&DJR No. 59, was renumbered 4559 when taken into LM&S stock in 1930 and finally allocated the number seen here under the system introduced by BR following Nationalisation in 1948. Here was an occasion which serves as an example of when Norman Lockett was unable to record the number of the Stanier 'Black 5'; no doubt because of the speed of the train and also because the heavy, hand-held, quarter-plate press camera proved too unwieldy to also permit observing and writing down the details of both locomotives! *18th April 1949*

SECTION 3
1948 TO 1952
NATIONALISATION – AND SOME RATIONALISATION

On 6th August 1947, the Transport Act received the Royal Assent. Included in its provisions, the railways of Great Britain were transferred into state ownership from 1st January 1948, for which purpose the British Transport Commission (BTC) was established and 'British Railways' came into being. Under the terms of the new Act, the BTC delegated many of the railway managerial and operating functions to a newly created Railway Executive. In turn, the Executive would oversee and coordinate a regional organisation, under which the day-to-day operations of the railways within the individual regions would be run. Stage one of the organisation consisted of the creation of six provisional regions which, as far as the future of the S&D was concerned, included a Western Region, a Southern Region and a London Midland Region. In effect, these new regions corresponded, at least initially, to the former systems of the GWR, the SR and to those parts of the LM&SR within England and Wales. Joint lines were to be merged into one of the regions.

As such, from 2nd February 1948, the S&D line was placed under the control of the Southern Region. Bath, however, was assigned to the LM Region, which remained responsible for the provision of motive power to the S&D. The locomotive stock allocated to the S&D sheds continued to display allegiance to the former LM&S Bristol District (the '22' group).

By the end of 1948, the Railway Executive had confirmed the first of its plans for a programme of 'inter-regional adjustments', reallocating those routes and stations on lines which 'penetrated' from one region across the boundary of another. The S&D was an obvious example, although it was not listed in the first announcement. However, one such adjustment which would affect the S&D was the transfer, from the LMR to the WR, of the commercial management of former LM&S lines south of Selly Oak to Bristol and Bath. Nevertheless, for practical reasons (including costs), it was accepted that the operating arrangements of many such lines, including motive power, would need to remain as before.

By January 1950, the boundaries of the new regions were confirmed. As relevant to the S&D line, one boundary between the WR and SR now ran parallel with and just to the south of the WR London, via Westbury, to Exeter main line. As such, the commercial responsibilities of the S&D were divided between the two regions, with the line northwards from (and including) Cole passing to the WR and the rest, running southwards, remaining with the SR. The latter, however, operated the entire S&D and, from February 1950, took over responsibility for the motive power, with the stock provided 'on loan' by the LMR. The locomotives now started to receive shed codes in the '71' group (the Eastleigh District). All very confusing; still in effect a Joint line but, significantly, with the Western Region now in commercial control of the northern half of the S&D.

With the S&D line entering the 1950s, Nationalisation was soon followed by some rationalisation, none of which was to be entirely unexpected. Prior to the Second World War, only a short section of the original S&D main line, serving Wimborne, had been lifted. Even then, much of that section of the line had been retained as a siding leading from Corfe Mullen to serve a local clay works. First, came the closure of Templecombe Lower Yard in 1950. The following year witnessed – in late October – the withdrawal of all traffic on the Glastonbury to Wells branch. On the same day, regular passenger traffic ceased to run on the section of the line between Highbridge and Burnham. In this latter case, however, summer

excursion trains continued to run over this short section until 1962. On 1st December 1952, passenger trains were withdrawn from the Edington Junction to Bridgwater branch, full closure following less than two years later. However, on the main line, summer traffic was reaching a post-war zenith, whilst freight was still the major week-day feature of the route, certainly between Bath and Evercreech Junction, all of which were to provide some very interesting years for the lineside enthusiast.

THE 'CLEETHORPES'

No. 233, 6.52 a.m. CLEETHORPES to BOURNEMOUTH WEST
No. 268, 10.40 a.m. BOURNEMOUTH WEST to NOTTINGHAM and CLEETHORPES

Owing to partial collapse of Arley Tunnel and the consequent blockage of the L.M.R. line from Leicester to Birmingham, the above-mentioned services will not operate as arranged this summer.

In order, however, to provide for Leicester and district passengers, the " Cleethorpes " train will start from Leicester at 9.28 a.m., and run via Market Harboro', Rugby and Birmingham (New Street), leaving there at 11.27 as booked, arriving Bath at 1.58 p.m., forward 2.12 p.m. to Bournemouth West, as shown in Working Time Table.

The 10.40 a.m. Bournemouth West to Nottingham and Cleethorpes will terminate at Nottingham at 5.37 p.m., but there will be a service forward from Nottingham to Cleethorpes by the 4.45 p.m. ex Birmingham, which arrives Nottingham at 6.53 p.m.

For the Leicester and district passengers travelling by the 10.40 a.m. a stop will be made at Burton, and a special service run from that station to Leicester, due 5.50 p.m.

The through rail service between Birmingham and Leicester is suspended and passengers are being conveyed over this section of the line as follows :—

Rail—Birmingham and stations to Arley and Fillongley.
Road—Arley and Fillongley, Stockingford and Nuneaton (Abbey Street).
Rail—Nuneaton (Abbey Street) and stations to Leicester.

It will be some time before through working is restored.   (23.5.49)

At the start of the summer timetable for 1949, a through service was advertised from Cleethorpes to Bournemouth, running via the S&D line. In effect, this was a summer Saturdays only extension of a weekday Cleethorpes to Birmingham service, leaving the North Lincolnshire seaside town at 6.52am. Arrival at Bournemouth, after a journey of about 309 miles occupying just four minutes short of ten hours (!), was scheduled as 4.48pm. The reporting number in the S&D Working Timetable was shown as '223'. However, before the new service had even commenced, fate was destined to take a hand. Arley Tunnel, on the route, between Nuneaton and Birmingham, suffered a partial collapse and alternative arrangements were put in hand (LEFT). This had no direct effect on the running over the S&D but instead of the 'Down Cleethorpes', we see here train 'M223' as the 9.28am Nottingham-Bournemouth, emerging from Winsor Hill Tunnel behind ex-MR Class '2P' No. 509 and a Stanier Class '5' 4-6-0 . *2nd July 1949*

WINSOR HILL

The twin railway tunnels under Winsor Hill (as generally referred to by the S&D) or Windsor Hill (as more often quoted by the Ordnance Survey), were sometimes also known as Downside Tunnels. The latter was a reference to the proximity of Downside Quarry which, as already noted in an earlier caption, was linked to the S&D until early 1940. Class '4F' 0-6-0 No. 4561, the last of the five 'Armstrongs' built especially for the S&D, had just emerged with the 9.05am Bristol Temple Meads-Bournemouth semi-fast service from the original 242 yards long single line tunnel, which dated from the opening of the line in 1874. A separate tunnel, a little to the left of the original (as viewed here from the south) was only 132 yards long and built to accommodate the Up line when this section of the S&D was doubled in 1892. Hence the impression gained from many of the pictures taken here that the train was running on a single line section whereas, as can just be seen in Norman's photograph, the Up line diverged away from the Down line for a short distance on either side of the tunnels. Incidentally, notice how, in the right background, the railway boundary fence and telegraph route were both taken in a straight line across the top of Winsor Hill, before dropping back down towards the formation level on the north side of the tunnel. *18th April 1949*

RIGHT: S&D passenger train loadings (main line), reproduced from the *Appendix to the Working Time Tables* – 1st January 1933, until further notice.

LOADING TABLE OF PASSENGER TRAINS.

Engines are classified, and bear a classification plate on the cabside.

CLASS OF ENGINE.	LOADED COACHES BETWEEN		
	Bath and Evercreech Junction.	Evercreech Junction and Bailey Gate including Templecombe Upper.	Bailey Gate and Bournemouth.
No. 1 class	130 tons	200 tons	175 tons
No. 2 class	190 tons	290 tons	260 tons
No. 4 class freight	230 tons	350 tons	310 tons
No. 7 class freight	310 tons	450 tons	415 tons
Engines Nos. 301, 302, 303, 320 and 321 ..	160 tons	245 tons	215 tons

In case of empty coaches or pigeon specials 20 tons may be added to the above figures.

Bank or assisting engines must not be taken with these loads unless through very bad weather or other exceptional causes.

When working passenger and milk trains between Highbridge and Templecombe the full load of a No. 1 class engine is 250 tons.

The loading limit for a Stanier Class '5' for the section of the line over the Mendips was set at 270 tons, roughly the equivalent of a maximum of eight coaches. An abundance of motive power, as witnessed here, possibly explained why such rapid progress was being achieved; a wonderful spectacle as both engines climbed the 1 in 50 gradient at speed on the approach to Winsor Hill Tunnel with the 2.45pm (SO) Bournemouth West-Bristol Temple Meads. The Class '2P' 4-4-0, No. 40564, had received a recent overhaul and a new livery in partially lined black, with the British Railways legend on the tender. The number of the Stanier 'Black Five' went unrecorded by Norman. The railway here was some 600 feet above sea level, having climbed about 400 feet since leaving Evercreech Junction. Ahead lay another two miles before the summit of the line was finally surmounted to the north of Masbury Halt. *2nd July 1949*

If you have ever listened to the sound recordings made by Peter Handford (who, sadly, died whilst this book was in preparation) and originally marketed on the 'Argos' label, this is the location where some of his best recordings of traffic over the S&D were made, although he was near the southern portal of the tunnel. A succession of Up trains can be heard whilst on the long climb from Shepton, the pilot or train engine whistling on the approach to the tunnel. In the background, a thunderstorm brews (in summer, quite a common occurrence amongst the Mendip Hills), whilst the sound of blasting can be heard from a nearby quarry north of the tunnel. Wonderfully evocative stuff for those who can still recall the real thing!

IN & OUT OF COMBE DOWN TUNNEL

Somewhere in this book – and this is as good a page as any – I wanted to clarify a couple of sometimes misquoted facts regarding Combe Down Tunnel. The first is the correct spelling; not Coombe Down, an error, as far as I can determine, that originated in the early 1950s with a well-known railway publishing house and which is sometimes still replicated in print today!

The second fact concerns the length of the tunnel, occasionally misquoted (including once by this writer!) as 1,826 yards rather than the correct figure of 1,829 yards. The difference occurs, I suspect, because distances measured on railways were generally quoted '*to the nearest chain*' – in the case of Combe Down Tunnel, 1 mile and 3 chains. The actual length (according to official drawings) is 1 mile, 3 chains, and 15 links. Now, those readers long enough in the tooth to remember good old imperial measurements will know that a chain equals 22 yards, and comprises 100 links. So 1 mile and 3 chains gives a total length of 1,826 yards whereas the addition of those 15 links (each 0.22 yard long) increases the total to 1,829 yards, or 1829 yards 10.8 inches if you wish to split hairs! *QED.*

A newcomer to the S&D. Ivatt Class '4MT' 2-6-0 No. 43012, allocated new to Bristol in April 1948, had been used occasionally over the S&D during that summer. The following year, this locomotive plus No's 43017 and 43036 were transferred to Bath. In effect, they replaced the Horwich 'Crabs' which had seen service on the line for the previous few years (a class of locomotive which appears to have escaped the attention of Norman Lockett). With the original double-chimney design (seen here, as fitted to the first fifty in the Ivatt class), their performance over the Mendip Hills was, at best, erratic. As such, having first been used on through traffic, they tended to be employed mainly for piloting work or, as on this occasion, local passenger services. Approaching Combe Down Tunnel with the 2.25pm stopping train from Templecombe to Bath, the rather austere appearance of these locomotives was emphasised when observed from a low angle. However, features such as the high running plate would soon become commonplace, as the various BR Standard classes were rolled out and placed into service from January 1951. *3rd August 1949*

Turning to look in the opposite direction from the previous view, some twenty-five minutes later, 0-6-0 No. 43875 emerged from Combe Down Tunnel with the 9.35am Bradford-Bournemouth West. This locomotive, designed by Henry Fowler, was one of the 192 built from 1911 as the first examples of what became the standard Midland Railway and, later, LM&SR Class '4F' 0-6-0. *3rd August 1949*

Norman's low level view here gives a good impression of the steepness of the southern flank of Combe Down, with only a short distance between the tunnel portal, cut deep into the hillside, and where the line then emerges from the cutting which follows. I have always marvelled at those who, by traversing the land on horseback and on foot, surveyed and selected the route from Midford to join the Midland Railway at Bath. An Act of Parliament in 1891, which gave approval to double the section of line between Wellow and Midford, also included extending the second set of rails northwards to this point immediately to the south of Combe Down Tunnel. There was even talk of a small station to serve the residents of 'the Down' and the village of Monkton Combe, which lies about a mile to the east. Land was purchased and Tucking Mill Viaduct widened but no further track was put down. At the end of the 1890s, the S&D Joint Committee had also considered doubling the full length of the single line between Midford and Bath Junction but the tremendous cost of enlarging the two tunnels was too much to justify the expenditure, so the four mile section was destined always to remain as a single track bottleneck.

Like many of the best of the numerous scenic locations through which the S&D wove its course, the lineside here could only be approached on foot, either by a climb from Tucking Mill, just a short distance further south (where the line was carried high above the foot of Horsecombe Vale), or via a long steep path leading down from Summer Lane, way above on the hillside of Combe Down. However, as can be judged from this and the other photographs Norman took at this location, the effort was always well worthwhile.

Some designs might come and soon depart from the S&D scene but the bark of an S&D Class '7F' 2-8-0 could be heard echoing across Horsecombe Vale for some fifty years from 1914, at which date the first six of the class were delivered new from Derby, to 1964, when the last was finally withdrawn from service. Here, No. 53801 attacks with vigour the climb from Midford with the 3.10pm freight from Evercreech Junction to Bath. Having just crossed Tucking Mill Viaduct (only the parapets of which can be seen here), the train is about to enter the confines of Combe Down Tunnel. This looks to be a loading well within the capabilities of the locomotive which, showing a clean exhaust, suggests there would be little difficulty encountered in completing the northbound ascent from Midford. The climb here was at its steepest, 1 in 50 for about 10 chains. Then, shortly after entering the southern portal of the tunnel, the gradient changed to and remained at 1 in 100 until the summit was reached within the confines of the tunnel, less than 350 yards before the northern portal, in Lyncombe Vale. *7th August 1949*

SOUTH OF MIDSOMER NORTON

Right on schedule, Class '4F' 0-6-0 No. 44422 climbs towards Chilcompton with the 4.25pm semi-fast from Bath to Bournemouth. Norman Lockett had this recorded as the 3.25pm ex-Bristol but, during the summer months only for a number of years, this service started from Gloucester. Note the gradient post in the foreground. This indicated a brief easing in the gradient for southbound trains from 1 in 53 to 1 in 60, then to 1 in 88, before hardening again to 1 in 50, the latter being the ruling gradient for the Bath Extension. *19th July 1950*

Class '2P' 4-4-0 No. 40634 and an unrecorded 'Black Five' 4-6-0 are nearly three miles into the southbound climb across the Mendips with the 'Pines Express', as they pound up the long straight from Midsomer Norton station. This part of the climb was an unrelenting gradient at 1 in 53 for about a mile and a quarter beyond Midsomer Norton. *15th May 1951*

Ivatt Class '4MT' 2-6-0 No. 43017 emerges from the 66 yards Chilcompton Tunnel with the 3.10pm stopping service from Bath to Templecombe. The tunnel is another reminder that, when this section of the line was doubled, a second bore (to accommodate the Up line) was constructed alongside the original single-line bore through which the train here is passing. The Ivatt 'Moguls' are, apparently, known today as 'Flying Pigs'; pigs they may have been but when on the S&D they were generally referred to as 'Doodlebugs' which those with long enough memories may recall was the name given in 1944 to the German V-1 flying bombs! *7th August 1951*

For those interested in a more detailed account of the performance of these Ivatt 2-6-0s whilst on the S&D, O.S. Nock reported on a couple of footplate journeys in his book Four Thousand Miles on the Footplate. It was evident that it was the demands made by the S&D route on the continuous steaming capacity of these locomotives which proved to be their shortcoming, a feature which, apparently, was overcome by the fitting of a single blastpipe and chimney. However, whilst none were ever destined to return to the S&D as the consequence of such modifications, the BR equivalent design – the Standard Class '4' 2-6-0s – were to become a regular sight.

Less than 100 yards to the south of the previous shot, Class '2P' 4-4-0 No. 40563 and Class '4F' 0-6-0 No. 44561 (ex-S&D No. 61) with the 3.25pm Gloucester-Bournemouth. This service was booked to run non-stop from Bath to Shepton Mallet and, when recorded here, some twenty minutes after leaving Bath, was running just a few minutes behind schedule. Nearly two years after the start of the BR era, the Class '4F' still carries 'LMS' on the tender side, whereas the leading locomotive has been through the paintshop and given a partially lined black livery, with the full 'BRITISH RAILWAYS' legend on the tender. *30th May 1950*

REDAN BRIDGE

This is Bridge No. 51, 'Redan Bridge', where, rather unusually, the parapet railings were clad with corrugated iron sheeting. The 3.10pm Bath-Templecombe features again and with another of the S&D 'Armstrongs' in charge, this time No. 44559. Unlike the summer Saturday through traffic, the gradients over the Mendip Hills presented no real challenge to the motive power when working a lightly loaded local passenger train. Just ahead of the '4F' lay the rock cutting through which the line passed on the approach to Chilcompton station, some 14½ miles and 46 minutes from the terminus at Bath. An average speed of 20mph was typical of S&D stopping traffic but what a wonderful way to enjoy the pleasures of the passing scenery! Incidentally, you will notice that references to Bath Midland station do not yet refer to the familiar distinguishing title 'Green Park', as this was not added by British Railways until the start of the summer season on 18th June 1951. *30th May 1950*

This is an early example of Norman Lockett using film negative instead of his preferred medium. David is uncertain whether his father was just experimenting, or (more likely) experiencing temporary problems obtaining his usual supply of glass plates. This may explain why this picture is a little 'on the skew' (the track was not on such a severe cant as suggested here!), a fault which our publisher has been unable to correct by rotating the scanned image, as this would result in 'losing' the bottom of the leading wheels of No. 44559. The fact that Norman captured so little of the foreground beneath the locomotive also suggests that he was yet to fully appreciate the difference between his usual larger format glass plates and the much smaller area of a roll film negative, the use of which, David seems to recall, required the fitting of an adaptor to his father's camera!

Reference has already been made to the minutiae included in the *Somerset & Dorset Appendix to the Working Time Tables*, which provided information and instruction for the 'Committee's servants'. Much of this information continued to appear in print into the BR era and until closure of the line – although by this time the 'Committee's servants' had become the railway's employees! As an example, the line between Midsomer Norton and Chilcompton included one of several locations where the local hunt, the Mendip Hunt, was allowed to cross the railway on the level, as witnessed by the following entry taken from the *Western Region Sectional Appendix to the WTT* for the Bristol Traffic District, as issued in October 1960. (The distances shown are from Bath Junction, where the S&D line joined the former Midland Railway.)

HOUNDS ON THE LINE.

Authority has been given to the Mendip Hunt to use the undermentioned level crossings between Midsomer Norton South and Shepton Mallet (Charlton Road) and train crews must be on the alert accordingly:—

Mileage		Stations between
m.	ch.	
12	50	.... Midsomer Norton South and Chilcompton.
14	12¾	.... Chilcompton and Binegar.
14	41	.... Chilcompton and Binegar.
19	25	.... Masbury Halt and Shepton Mallet (Charlton Road).
20	40½	.... Masbury Halt and Shepton Mallet (Charlton Road).

MAIN LINE FREIGHT

S&D Class '7'F 2-8-0 No. 53808, one of the class which still retained the 5ft 3ins diameter type G9BS boiler, climbs the long 1 in 50 gradient towards Winsor Hill Tunnel. The train is the 3.10pm Evercreech Junction to Bath freight, a service which was scheduled for the assistance of a banker, thus requiring a pause at Binegar for the banker to be detached. On this occasion, however, it looks as though No. 53808 is working the train within the limits of a 'single load', so no banking assistance was necessary. Northwards from Binegar, the freight then called, as necessary, at Chilcompton, Midsomer Norton and Radstock, primarily to drop off empty coal wagons for the collieries. No. 53808 continued to run with the boiler seen here for only two more years. A visit to Derby in late 1953 resulted in the provision of a type G9AS boiler, as per the original 1914-built locomotives of this class. *18th July 1951*

No. 53808, carrying the type G9AS boiler, is the locomotive which, in 1969, was purchased for £2,500 (on hire purchase terms!) by the S&DR Circle (later becoming the S&DR Trust) from Dai Woodham at Barry and taken to the Circle's base at Radstock to commence restoration. When the Radstock site had to be vacated, the locomotive was moved in January 1976, again by rail, to the West Somerset Railway to complete restoration to full running order; this was achieved in 1987. After 8¾ years in use by the WSR, No. 53808 underwent another major restoration between 1996 and late 2005, since when she has run in S&D Prussian Blue livery and bearing her original number 88. Although never carried in her working life, the blue livery (an anathema to the purists but, hey, it's only a coat of paint!) has proved very popular with visitors young and old to the WSR. The Trust has secured the longer term future of its locomotive by means of a full repairing lease to the WSR plc until 30th April 2020.

On looking back through the numerous references to the S&D 2-8-0s, there appears to be unamity that the diameter of the non-standard Type G9BS boiler (as originally carried by the five 1925 locomotives and as still seen on No. 53808 above) was 5 ft 3 inches. However, as regards the Type G9AS carried by the first six members of the class (dating from 1914) and, eventually by all eleven locomotives, I have seen variously quoted diameters of 4ft $7^1/_8$ ins, 4 ft 8ins, 4ft $8^1/_8$ ins and 4ft $9^1/_8$ ins! (The latter used by Ivo Peters). But were they all quoting from a common basis? Having consulted the expert team on all S&DJR locomotive matters, Gerry Nichols assured me that the figure generally regarded as being the 'nominal diameter' is the 'barrel diameter outside first (ie. front) ring' which, for the Type G9AS was 4ft $7^1/_8$ins; so that's good enough for me and this tome! The figure as quoted by Ivo equates, I understand, to the 'barrel diameter outside rear ring'.

BRANCH LINE FREIGHT

As the late-afternoon shadows lengthen on a sunny autumn day, Class '3F' 0-6-0 No. 43204, running more than half an hour behind schedule, eases the 11.15am freight from Evercreech Junction through Highbridge East station. The lengthy goods is about to cross the WR main line in order to reach its destination, half a mile further west, at Highbridge Wharf. What better an introduction to Norman Lockett's return to the Highbridge area. *11th October 1950*

RETURN TO HIGHBRIDGE

s seen earlier, Norman Lockett had taken his very first photographs (just the two!) of the S&D at Highbridge in April 1935 and it was to be another 15½ years before he returned here with his camera. Interestingly, his visit in 1950 was during a couple of days in early October, perhaps using a part of his annual holiday entitlement, some of which his employer may have required to be taken outside the traditional holiday period. Perhaps, however, he chose to come back because he knew the passenger services over the short section of the line between Highbridge and Burnham were at risk. Likewise, he returned again in the same month the following year, when the fate of the services to Burnham

had been confirmed. The latter visits took place just a few weeks before the regular passenger services were withdrawn although, as mentioned earlier, right up until September 1962, a few services and excursion trains were run through to Burnham during some Bank Holidays and in the height of the summer season. In making his visits during 1950-51, Norman captured some wonderful scenes of this little-photographed part of the S&D, when the local services were still in the hands of elderly Johnson 0-4-4Ts and 0-6-0s, both types traditionally associated with the S&D. Indeed, apart from the numbers and the livery carried, many of the scenes Norman photographed here must have been little changed from those of fifty years earlier.

Johnson 0-4-4T No. 58046, at the end of the five minute journey with the 2.35pm from Burnham on Sea, rests at Highbridge. To be accurate, Highbridge East, the title only then recently bestowed on the former S&D station by British Railways to distinguish it from the adjoining ex-GW station, which forthwith carried the suffix 'West'. This locomotive, originally No. 1644 and built at Derby in 1884, was renumbered as No. 1298 in 1907. Renumbered yet again, No. 58046 returned to Highbridge in August 1949 following a stay at Bristol, Barrow Road, during which the Class '1P' had been repaired, at least partially repainted and lined out in the new BR livery. She was withdrawn and sent to Derby for cutting up towards the end of 1951. *11th October 1950*

Running about twenty minutes early, 0-6-0 Class '3F' No. 43792 eases the 11.15am freight from Evercreech Junction past the former S&D Carriage & Wagon Works at Highbridge, the north side of which can just be seen on the extreme right of this view. The footplate crew appear to be driver Charlie King and fireman Les Warren, who are about to take their train through the station and across the GW main line, before completing the final half a mile to reach the sidings at Highbridge Wharf. Norman took this picture from the east end of the Up through platform (numbered platform 5 in BR days). The old C&W Works were severely damaged by fire later in the 1950s and what remained of this structure was soon demolished. The sidings seen in the left background were retained for carriage storage. *11th October 1950*

BURNHAM

BANK HOLIDAY MONDAY, 1st AUGUST—*continued*

HALF-DAY EXCURSION, TEMPLECOMBE TO BURNHAM-ON-SEA AND BACK

Forward	M.543 a.m. arr.	dep.	Return	M.543 p.m. arr.	dep.
Templecombe Upper	...	11 1	Burnham-on-Sea	...	7 30
Wincanton	11 7	11 10	Highbridge	7 35	7 36
Cole	11 18	11 20	Bason Bridge	7 40	7 41
Evercreech Junction	11 26	11 30	Edington Burtle	7 48	7 49
Pylle	11 35	11 36	Shapwick	7 54	7 55
West Pennard	11 43	11 44	Ashcott	7 59	8 0
Glastonbury	11 53	11 55	Glastonbury	8 6	8 10
Ashcott	12 1	12 2	West Pennard	8 19	8 20
Shapwick	12 6	12 7	Pylle	8 29	8 30
Edington Burtle	12 12	12 13	Evercreech Junction	8 35	8 40
Bason Bridge	12 21	12 22	Cole	8 46	8 47
Highbridge	12 26	12 27	Wincanton	8 55	8 57
Burnham-on-Sea	12 32	...	Templecombe Upper	9 5	...

10 S.R. coaches, 310 tons.

9.55 a.m. Evercreech Junction to Highbridge will be extended to Burnham-on-Sea, as under:
Highbridge dep. 10.55 a.m.
Burnham-on-Sea arr. 11.0 a.m.
7.5 p.m. Highbridge to Evercreech Junction will start from Burnham-on-Sea as under:
Burnham-on-Sea dep. 6.45 p.m.
Highbridge arr. 6.50 p.m. Forward as booked.

STRENGTHENING BRANCH LINE TRAINS

7.0 a.m. and 4.15 p.m. Highbridge and Burnham-on-Sea to be strengthened by **one extra coach** to work with set for remainder of day.
9.55 a.m. Evercreech Junction to Highbridge and Burnham-on-Sea will be strengthened by **five extra coaches** to return by 7.5 p.m. Highbridge and Burnham-on-Sea to Evercreech Junction.

Burnham, or Burnham-on-Sea (a courtesy title which appears to have been bestowed on the small railway terminus during the early 1920s) originally comprised a short single platform, part of which was enclosed by a train shed with an overall roof. This, no doubt, was a feature much appreciated by passengers seeking shelter from the winds and rain blowing off the nearby Bristol Channel. The shoreline lay less than 200 yards away and, originally, the railway extended via a steep gradient onto a stone pier projecting through the mudflats on the estuary of the River Parrett. This was all part of the long-abandoned grandiose scheme to link South Wales to Highbridge by steamship, then via the S&D to Hamworthy (Poole) to connect with a shipping service across the English Channel to France.

Norman Lockett took just two photographs here (both of the same train!), positioning himself on the excursion platform, a lengthy pre-cast concrete structure – with no protection for passengers. This second platform had been added to the original facilities in anticipation of the large number of excursionists who, it was hoped, might be attracted to Burnham. Class '1P' 0-4-4T No. 58046 prepares to leave with the 4.00pm train to Evercreech Junction, a journey of 24¼ miles which would occupy an hour and ten minutes to complete. When Norman first visited the area in 1935, there was still a daily passenger service comprising some twenty arrivals at and departures from Burnham, many of which ran only the 1¾ miles to and from Highbridge. By 1950, the last full year of regular traffic, this had reduced to less than half the pre-war level. *10th October 1950*

HIGHBRIDGE
CHURCH STREET
CROSSING

The first three-quarters of a mile westwards from the S&D station formed a part of the original Somerset Central Railway (SCR), which linked Glastonbury to a wharf on the River Brue. This section was opened to traffic on 28th August 1854. In 1858, the SCR extended about a mile and a quarter further to Burnham, on the Bristol Channel, where a slipway was built to enable a shipping service to provide a link to and from South Wales. On leaving Highbridge station, and having crossed the GWR Bristol to Exeter main line on the level, the 1858 extension formed a junction with and ran parallel to the earlier SCR line as far as Highbridge Wharf, before heading off north-westwards for the remainder of the short journey to the little terminus and slipway at Burnham.

A superb study at a little-photographed location, where the railway crossed Church Street on the level in Highbridge. This, the route of the A38, was the main road from Bristol to the West of England before the opening of the M5 motorway. On the east side of the level crossing, a footbridge had been provided for pedestrians unwilling to wait the passage of a train and the reopening of the gates. The bridge also provided a convenient position from which to photograph the railway. Highbridge East 'A' Signal Box, on the opposite side of the road, controlled the gates and the lines to Burnham and to the Wharf. Formerly, Highbridge 'C' Signal Box, this attractive little structure with its external balcony had been renamed from 26th September 1949. The photograph gives the impression that this is a double track section but the righthand set of rails is the single line between Highbridge and Burnham, whilst that on the left was the goods line serving Highbridge Wharf. The railway crossed Church Street between 'The Lamb' on the left, a public house in the ownership of that once familiar West Country brewery – Starkey, Knight & Ford Ltd – and the Regal cinema on the right, at the junction with Newtown Road, which ran parallel to the north boundary of the railway. In 1950-51, Highbridge shed was home to four of the Johnson Class '1P' 0-4-4Ts, these being No's 58046/7/88 and, seen here approaching the crossing with the 4.0pm Burnham to Evercreech Junction train, No. 58086. This engine was an example of the final version of these 0-4-4Ts to be built, one of a batch of twenty constructed by Dübs & Co. in 1900 and allocated No. 2623. Renumbered as No. 1423 in 1907, the locomotive was rebuilt with a Belpaire boiler and was subsequently motor fitted for push/pull services. As we will see later, No. 58086 was destined to become the last of the class to be withdrawn. *2nd October 1951*

This is the view from Church Street level crossing pedestrian footbridge looking in the opposite direction (eastwards), towards the WR main line, beyond which was Highbridge East station. Class '3F' 0-6-0 No. 43792 had arrived with the 11.15am freight from Evercreech Junction and was held waiting to cross the main road in order to enter the sidings at Highbridge Wharf. Until the route could be set for the train to proceed, the points in the foreground, ahead of the 0-6-0, were set for a short 'trap' siding which terminated in a set of buffers abutting the footbridge. The large brick-built structure on the right was the S&D goods shed, to which access by road vehicles was gained from Market Street. The plate carried on a short post adjacent to the near corner of the shed indicated 'Bridge No. 282', an underground culvert which carried a watercourse beneath the railway at this point. *12th October 1950*

Many years ago, whilst researching my television series about 'The Branch', I was informed by an elderly Highbridge resident that the bungalow, seen to the left of this photograph, had been owned by the S&D and used as living accommodation. Whilst I have never discovered any documentary evidence in support of this, the building did stand very close to the lineside and pedestrian access appeared to be via the foot crossing over the running lines at the far end of the goods shed.

OUT AND BACK

No. 58047 features here as the third of the quartet of Johnson 0-4-4Ts based at Highbridge at the time Norman Lockett made his visits in 1950/1. The locomotive was built at Derby in 1884, entering service as MR No. 1649 but was renumbered in 1907 as No. 1303. Now carrying the number allocated by BR, this locomotive was the last of the Highbridge allocation to retain a round-topped firebox and Salter safety valves. She was withdrawn from service in July 1952 and sent to Derby for scrapping. In the picture, ABOVE, No. 58047 approaches Church Street level crossing with the 3.38pm Highbridge to Burnham-on-Sea, whilst BELOW, some twenty-five minutes later, she makes the return journey in charge of the 4.05pm Burnham to Evercreech Junction. In this second view, note the signal post carrying two arms facing in opposite directions. Now look carefully at the upper picture and this same signal post and arms can just be seen in the distance. The lower arm was the Up distant for Highbridge East 'A' Signal Box, the upper arm being the Down home for the 'B' box. The 'B' box controlled access to the S&D goods loop and sidings, and a level crossing over the access road to the WR goods yard. Here, No. 58047 has slowed and is approaching the crossing with the WR main line prior to entering the S&D station. *6th October 1951*

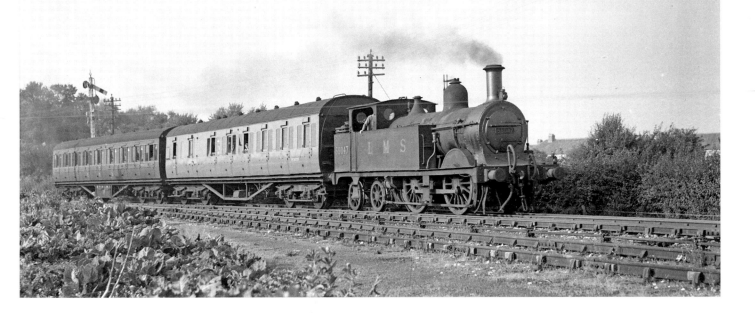

Here we have the fourth and last example of the 1950-51 Highbridge allocation of the elderly Johnson 0-4-4T locomotives. No. 58088, seen about to depart Highbridge with the 2.05pm Burnham to Templecombe service, was another example of the final version of the class to be built, details of which have been given already. Allocated No. 2625 when first entering service and renumbered as No. 1425 in 1907, this member of the class had been rebuilt with a type G5½ Belpaire boiler. By comparing this photograph of No. 58088 with that seen earlier featuring No. 58086, it will be observed that those responsible for repainting these locomotives had yet to implement a standard BR livery for this class of 0-4-4Ts. *10th October 1950*

FREIGHT TO THE WHARF

Class '3F' 0-6-0 No. 43792 was obviously a regular performer with the Highbridge 'Market', the 11.15am Evercreech-Highbridge Wharf freight. This was allowed four hours in the Working Timetable to complete the twenty-three mile journey, calling at many of the intermediate stations. On this occasion, however, the train was approaching the Wharf an hour ahead of schedule. This was a regular practice on the S&D, allowing freight to run 'ahead of time' providing this did not adversely affect any other traffic. By the start of the 1950s, Highbridge Wharf had ceased to handle any sea-borne traffic but the sidings remained in use to serve some local trade, and for the storage and sorting of wagons, including transfers to and from the WR yard. *2nd October 1951*

COAL FOR BURNHAM

No. 43216 crosses over from the Goods line to gain the single line to Burnham with a couple of wagons of coal destined, no doubt, for a merchant trading out of the small goods yard at the seaside terminus. No. 43216 was another of the Johnson 0-6-0s built for the S&D. It was the first of five constructed by Neilson Reid & Co. in 1902, delivered as S&DJR No. 72 and renumbered by the LM&S as No. 3216. She was the last of the S&D 'Bulldogs' to work on the line, remaining in service until August 1962. *6th October 1951*
The section of the line between Highbridge East 'A' (formerly Highbridge 'C') Signal Box and Burnham was worked by means of the 'train staff & ticket' system, the only section on the Somerset & Dorset Railway to retain this method of block working after 1895. The short section between Highbridge East 'A' and East 'B' boxes was worked on the 'no staff' system, which relied only on the block instruments and bells. One local source has been quoted as stating that only the block bell at both of the boxes was used but evidence of this has yet to be established.

The panoramic view eastwards from Highbridge East station footbridge. No. 43248, another of the Neilson Reid & Co. 0-6-0 locomotives (S&DJR No. 75 of 1902), is given the road to cross the WR main line and proceed with this freight service towards the sidings at the Wharf. Norman's view of the station included all five of the platform faces and at least one passenger! Beyond the station, in the mid-distance, Highbridge East 'C' Signal Box can be seen. It was renamed twice by BR in little more than a year – from Highbridge Loco, the original name, to Highbridge 'A' on 4th July 1948 and then to Highbridge East 'C' from 26th September 1949. *6th October 1951*

*Following the cessation of regular passenger traffic between Highbridge and Burnham, the Western Region amended the title of the station at the former to read 'Highbridge and Burnham-on-Sea'. Some years later, towards the end of the 1950s, some BR totems were provided on the platforms declaring the station to be 'Highbridge **for** Burnham on Sea', perhaps a more accurate description.*

NEWBRIDGE ACCOMMODATION CROSSING

ABOVE: Near Newbridge, about three-quarters of a mile east of Highbridge station, the S&D line bisected a narrow lane, or 'drove', for the continued usage of which an accommodation crossing had been provided by the railway company. Norman Lockett must have established, either from the train or – more likely – from an OS map, that this would be a suitable lineside location at which he could take these three photographs. No. 58088 is featured again with the 2.05pm Burnham to Templecombe service, accelerating away from Highbridge and heading for a first station stop at Bason Bridge, less than a mile further along the line. Looking westwards along the track, the disused buildings of the old S&D Works can be seen in the background. *11th October 1950*

Today, the view here towards Highbridge is obscured by the M5 motorway, which crosses over the trackbed of the S&D and the nearby River Brue. When I last visited this location there was, however, one reminder of the old railway – the arm of a distant signal, reputedly the Highbridge East C Box Up distant which had been sited nearby, was fixed to the wall of a former farmhouse.

OPPOSITE PAGE TOP: Looking in the opposite direction, eastwards towards Bason Bridge and Edington Junction, 0-4-4T No. 58046 approaches the crossing, bunker first, with the 1.15pm Evercreech Junction to Burnham-on-Sea. This location was, of course, a part of the very first section of what would become the S&DR; the 12¼ miles of single track built for the Somerset Central Railway, which opened to traffic between Highbridge and Glastonbury on 28th August 1854. Originally, this was a broad gauge line, a reminder of the fact that the SCR owed much of its very existence to the allegiance of the Bristol & Exeter Railway Company. *11th October 1950*

OPPOSITE PAGE BOTTOM: The Up distant signal for Highbridge East 'C' Box can be seen as 'Bulldog' 0-6-0 No. 43204 trundles past with the 11.15am Evercreech North Yard-Highbridge Wharf freight. This was another of the Johnson Class '3F' 0-6-0s which had been delivered new, as S&DJR No. 65, from Derby in 1896. Subsequently provided with a different style of boiler and later renumbered as No. 3204 by the LM&S in 1930, the locomotive remained on the S&D system long enough to pass into BR ownership. Renumbered again as seen here, within two years of the date of this photograph No. 43204 was allocated away from the line and was withdrawn in 1957. The nickname 'Bulldog' had been used on the S&D to describe these locomotives from an early date, an expression of their ruggedness and ability for hard work. It was a name which stuck and continued to be used until the last had been withdrawn. *11th October 1950*

THE BRIDGWATER BRANCH
OCTOBER 1951

Opened in 1890, the seven mile branch to Bridgwater had been promoted and built as an independent line. Leased to the S&DJR until absorbed by the L&SWR in 1921, the branch was, in all but legal title, always perceived as an integral, if insignificant, part of the S&D system. Leaving the Evercreech Junction to Burnham line at Edington Junction (previously Edington Road), the line crossed the Polden Hills calling at Cossington and, from 1923, Bawdrip Halt, before reaching the terminus. Proposals to close the line were first mooted as early as 1933, so it came as no major surprise when notice of closure of passenger traffic was issued in 1952. This took effect from 1st December 1952, whilst freight traffic lasted less than another two years, the line closing completely on 1st October 1954.

Perhaps aware that the end of passenger services was near, Norman Lockett paid three visits to the area (although not, it appears, to Bridgwater) in early and mid-October 1951. Following complete closure of the Bridgwater branch, the former junction station was renamed Edington Burtle. Edington Junction was another of those stations seemingly miles from any major habitation. Just up the road stood the local pub, the Station Hotel, whilst beyond was the small settlement of Burtle. Edington village lay 1½ miles across the moors to the south. When, some years ago, the author had the opportunity to interview a few of those who had worked at or used this lonely station, it was evident that the closure of the railway must have created much the same effect on the local community as we witness nowadays with the loss of a rural post office.

Johnson 0-4-4T No. 58088 arrives at Edington Junction with the 9.45am train from Burnham-on-Sea to Evercreech Junction. The train was due to pause here for two minutes to provide connections to and from the Bridgwater train. The signal box just features in the left foreground, provided when the branch line to Bridgwater was opened in July 1890. Beyond the box, 0-6-0 No. 43218, which had arrived with the 9.42am from Bridgwater, has run round its single coach train and is about to set back into the station bay platform, ready to form the 10.10am departure to Bridgwater. *2nd October 1951*

Class '3F' 0-6-0 No. 43218, sets off from Edington Junction with the 10.10am train to Bridgwater, a journey scheduled to take eighteen minutes. Views of Edington Junction station are few and far between, so it is disappointing that Norman's photograph has the locomotive with its single coach masking all of the station buildings. Indeed, the Bridgwater branch was a rarely photographed backwater, so these pictures of Norman's are an important record of its impending demise. No. 43218 was originally S&DJR No. 73, delivered new to the line in September 1902, another of the Neilson, Reid & Co. locomotives. She was withdrawn from service in April 1960. *2nd October 1951*

Exactly two weeks after his visit to Edington Junction, Norman Lockett returned to the branch. The authors believe that, on this occasion, he travelled by train to Cossington and then, perhaps, walked over the Polden Ridge to Bawdrip. Bawdrip Halt, between Cossington and Bridgwater, was not provided until July 1923, so it existed in use for only twenty-nine years. Norman recorded the time of this photograph as 4.0pm, so this must have been the 3.55pm Bridgwater North to Edington Junction train. This was scheduled as a mixed train but on this occasion there was obviously no goods traffic to add to the single carriage. The identity of the Class '3F' locomotive was unrecorded but it was possibly No. 43218 again. *16th October 1951*

This is Norman's only photograph taken at Cossington, a delightful shot of the road entrance to the station; it was very rare for Norman not to include a train but, perhaps, here he didn't get the opportunity or possibly something about this timeless scene just appealed to him. It was probably taken prior to the photograph at Bawdrip but, for layout purposes, has been included here after that view. The two-storey stone-built station house dominated the other accommodation. The buildings were an attractive design, built of the light-coloured local stone and with pantile roofs, the tiles presumably coming from Bridgwater, a centre for brick and tile manufacture. Note, too, the noticeboards, lettered 'S&DJ' RAILWAY' on the station wall. Cossington is, perhaps, best remembered – at least by enthusiasts – for the quirky footnote included for many years in S&D WTT which stated 'All Engines working passenger Trains not running Funnel first must stop at Cossington whether marked to do so or not'! 16th October 1951

Norman may have used his visit on 16th October to 'scout' a suitable lineside location because, the following day, he returned to take just this single photograph. It is one of the very few in this book which have been published previously but we make no apologies for including this splendid and rarely photographed scene as a final view of the Bridgwater branch, before returning you to the S&D main line. 'Bulldog' 0-6-0 No. 43218 climbs Cossington Bank with the 2.35pm from Edington Junction. Being a mixed train, conveying both passenger and freight traffic, this service was allowed 28 minutes to complete its journey rather than the customary 18 minutes. This was to allow 10 minutes for shunting, if required, at Cossington, during which operation any passengers were required to vacate the carriage! Bearing in mind that, by this date, there may have been, at best, half a dozen passengers, one wonders if this operating requirement was always honoured to the letter! *17th October 1951*

THE 'PINES EXPRESS'

We're back on the main line and I have to admit that this photograph came as rather a surprise to both of the authors – it is not the 'typical' Norman Lockett style of photograph! The Down 'Pines Express', having emerged from Devonshire Tunnel (notice the smoke still issuing from the southern portal), heads into the cutting leading under an accommodation bridge (Mogers Bridge) and towards the entrance to Combe Down Tunnel. Norman made no record of the motive power, which appears to be the usual combination allocated to this duty at the start of the 1950s, a Class '2P' 4-4-0 assisting a Stanier Class '5' 4-6-0. Both locomotives are working hard on the 1 in 50 gradient, the summit of which the train will reach before the entrance to Combe Down Tunnel. *2nd October 1950 The summit of the climb out of Bath has often been stated as a few feet after entering Combe Down Tunnel, whereas the gradient changed from 1 in 50 to level on reaching the three-arch underbridge (No. 14) just 2 chains **before** entering the northern portal of the tunnel.*

This more traditional and dramatic view depicts the Down 'Pines Express' in the same location as the previous picture. Class '2P' No. 40634 pilots an unidentified Stanier Class '5' across the three-arch Watery Bottom Bridge (Bridge No. 12), with both locomotives working flat out hauling this heavy train. Many of the carriages are in the new BR livery of crimson lake and cream (or 'plum and spilt milk' as it was sometimes called). Evidence of some recent spot re-sleepering can be seen at the side of the line, whilst the undergrowth on the side of the embankment, cut back so neatly the previous year, is showing the first signs of customary regrowth. *2nd May 1951*

THE S&D CLASS '7F' 2-8-0S (1925 SERIES)

As already mentioned, the second series of this famous class, comprising an additional five locomotives, was delivered in 1925. They were constructed by Robert Stephenson & Co. Ltd of Newcastle and allocated S&D No's 86-90. They differed from the original 1914 series by having a non-standard type G9BS 5ft 3ins diameter boiler, left-hand drive and various other modifications. By the end of 1930, two of these later-built engines had been given a smaller diameter type boiler equal to the earlier series.

By the start of the 1950s, the three remaining locomotives from the 1925 series, now numbered 53806-08, were still to be seen in action on the Somerset & Dorset retaining their large diameter boilers. Norman Lockett photographed two of the trio, as shown in this next sequence, but the other, No. 53807, appears to have eluded him.

Two of the local gangers stand outside their lineside hut as No. 53808 pounds up the final few yards towards Masbury Summit with the 11.20am Bath to Evercreech Junction freight. The efforts of the banking engine, giving essential assistance at the rear of this heavy train, are obscured by the exhaust of No. 53808. Notice how, despite all her hard work, the '7F' is still 'feathering' at the safety valve; the fireman (and the bank engine) has done a good job – no wonder the footplate crew appear so happy to be captured by Norman's photographic exploits! By the way, the various references to freight traffic running to or originating from Evercreech Junction should be interpreted as meaning Evercreech Junction North Yard. On arrival at 'the Junction', southbound freights terminating or calling at the North Yard would be set back onto the branch line, where the train engine was released and the yard pilot placed the stock into the appropriate siding, usually for remarshalling. *10th October 1949*
You may recall, I mentioned in the Introduction to this book that, first and foremost, Norman Lockett was very much an enthusiast of the Great Western Railway. His picture above reminds me of the following little anecdote as recounted to me many years ago by Ivo Peters. Norman was, by nature, a very placid man but one sure-fire method of raising his hackles was if Ivo dared to suggest that an S&D Class '7F' was far superior to a Great Western 2-8-0! As Ivo said, "It never failed – until Norman realised it was a wind-up!"

ABOVE: When measured overall of cladding, the difference in boiler diameter between the 1914 and 1925 series Class '7F' 2-8-0s was only about 7 inches, yet the later-build locomotives appeared massive (and so much more impressive!) especially, as here, when viewed from a low angle. No. 53806 makes light of this short freight, the 5.00pm from Bath, on the climb towards Chilcompton Tunnel. During the period 1953-55, all three of the 1925 series still retaining the larger boiler each came back from visits to works for repairs with the smaller boiler fitted, the last being No. 53806 at Derby in August 1955. *10th May 1950*

TUCKING MILL

After more than a mile of suffocating darkness, a whistle from the locomotive of a Down train heralded its emergence from the southern portal of Combe Down Tunnel into Horsecombe Vale. However, the rails of the Somerset & Dorset were not the first to pass through the pastoral splendour of this valley; more than sixty years before the S&D opened its line to the public, a tramway was constructed, as part of a scheme to convey stone from a quarry on Combe Down to a wharf on the Somersetshire Coal Canal at Tucking Mill. This had been proposed by William Smith who, in later years, gained fame as the 'Father of English Geology', having worked out the order and classification of rock formation, leading to the publication of his acclaimed *General Map of Strata found in England & Wales*.

Part of the course of the steeply sloping tramway is thought to have paralleled the route later adopted by the S&D northwards from Tucking Mill, before passing over the site of what became the southern portal of Combe Down Tunnel and climbing the steep hillside towards Smith's Quarry, near Summer Lane. However, this turned out to be a short-lived venture and the rails had long since disappeared by the time the S&D surveyors passed this way in the late 1860s, planning the route of the proposed railway which would link to the newly arrived Midland Railway at Bath.

ABOVE: The parapets of Tucking Mill Viaduct can just be seen in the background of this view, as Bulleid 'West Country' Class 4-6-2 No. 34037 *Clovelly*, which Norman recorded running exactly to time, climbs towards Combe Down Tunnel with the 3.35pm Bournemouth West-Bristol St. Philips. This service carried mail (hence the van at the rear of the train) for transfer, at Mangotsfield, to the 7.20pm Bristol-Newcastle postal service. *6th June 1951*
Following trials over the S&D in March 1951, the Southern Region transferred four of their 'Light Pacifics' – No's 34040 to 34043 – to Bath shed. In addition, other members of the class based at Bournemouth Central shed, started to become frequently seen on the route.

OPPOSITE PAGE BOTTOM: No. 53809, one of the 1925 series, was rebuilt with a smaller diameter boiler following a serious runaway accident in November 1929. The modification included the insertion of a distance piece in the smokebox saddle, which can be seen here as the locomotive climbs towards Chilcompton with the 5.15pm freight from Bath. The left-hand drive of the 1925 series was retained. The exhaust of the banking engine is just visible at the rear. *30th May 1950*
This is the second S&D Class '7F' returned to working order, after purchase from Woodham Bros in 1975 by Frank Beaumont. After full restoration as No. 13809, the locomotive made many main line steam runs. Now based at the Midland Railway Centre, Butterley, the 2-8-0 has again been fully overhauled and returned to steam, this time in BR black livery and carrying No. 53809. More recent highlights have included a nostalgic brief visit to the former Bath Green Park station and to the WSR where, during the 2006 Steam Gala, No. 53809 undertook some runs in tandem with No. 53808 (running as No. 88), the first pairing of two of the S&D '7Fs' since 1959.

Drifting down the gradient across Tucking Mill Viaduct, ex-MR Class '2P' 4-4-0 No. 40509, with Maunsell 3-set No. 393 already repainted in BR crimson and cream, heads for the first station call at Midford with the 4.35pm Bath-Templecombe. The rear of the train is just passing the Midford Down distant signal, which was located some 1,171 yards (just over ⁵/s of a mile) north of Midford Signal Box. *6th June 1951*

The viaduct (Bridge No. 16), ninety-six yards long and consisting of eight arches which carried the line more than sixty feet above the bottom of Horsecombe Vale, was originally a very spindly limestone structure, wide enough only to accommodate the single set of rails it carried, the stone most likely won when cutting Combe Down Tunnel. Upon the official Board of Trade inspection, it was one of several parts of the newly completed works which the Inspector advised must be carefully watched for some years to come! In the event, when some eighteen years later it was widened ready to receive double track, the original stonework was fully encased with railway brick and the arches strengthened. If you compare this scene (the views above and opposite) with Norman's photograph on page 19, you will note the brick-built refuges on the viaduct have been removed. They proved superfluous once the decision had been taken not to lay a second set of rails northwards from Midford and their removal, and replacement by horizontal bars to bridge the gaps in the brickwork, was probably undertaken to minimise future maintenance costs. Some years later, when the parapets to Midford Viaduct were renewed, the brick refuges there were similarly removed. Down below on either side of the viaduct, in the bottom of the vale, were situated the ponds and generally rather ramshackle buildings that had formed the Tucking Mill Works where, for very many years, Fuller's Earth* had been dried, processed, bagged and sent away, originally by way of the nearby Somersetshire Coal Canal and, later, via the S&D from Midford goods yard. This lay conveniently close at hand, just along the narrow lane linking Tucking Mill to Midford village.

* For readers wishing to learn much more of the history of the local Fuller's Earth Industry, a fascinating and detailed book, A History of The Fuller's Earth Mining Industry Around Bath *by Neil Macmillen & Mike Chapman, will be published by Black Dwarf Lightmoor Publications in late 2008.*

The guard of the 5.15pm Bath to Poole freight will have the brake in his van screwed on firmly and, despite the down grade, the driver of S&D class '7F' No. 53804 will be keeping sufficient steam on to ensure the couplings are well strained on emerging from Combe Down Tunnel, until passing Midford Signal Box. This procedure was one of a number of specific instructions to enginemen and guards for the working of S&D freight trains to minimise the risk of a 'snatch' and the possibility of a broken wagon coupling. *6th June 1951*

The southern portal of Combe Down Tunnel was located immediately beyond the lefthand edge of the photograph – just past the stone retaining arches which can be seen supporting the Down side of the cutting. It is thought that William Smith's tramway; to which I refer on page 75, having climbed from the Coal Canal, continued up the slope of Combe Down on a course parallel with the trees seen here behind the goods train, before following much the same route as the S&D boundary fence in the background. There remains some doubt, however, as to whether the tramway rails ever reached this far!

MOTIVE POWER – ANCIENT AND MODERN

No. 40505 hurries up the grade from Shepton Mallet and approaches Winsor Hill Tunnel. Norman Lockett recorded this as the 12.55pm Bournemouth-Bath, which on reaching Templecombe at 2.35pm, waited until 4.15pm before proceeding to Bath! Norman took the photograph at 3.35pm, so this is more likely the 2.25pm Templecombe to Bath, running about 15 minutes behind schedule. By the way, note the pipe emerging from the base of the smokebox, feeding the exhaust steam injector. Both of the former MR-built Class '2P' locomotives working on the S&D at this time, No's. 40505 and 40509, had been provided with this feature. *18th July 1951*

Providing a contrast to the erratic performance of the Ivatt 'Moguls' in the early 1950s (see caption and picture opposite), the S&D line retained the services of two elderly 4-4-0s of Midland Railway lineage. The first 4-4-0 appeared on the S&D in May 1891 and locomotives (both MR and LM&SR) of this wheel arrangement continued to serve the S&D with distinction into the early years of the 1960s. These two locomotives dated from 1899, having been built for the Midland Railway by Sharp Stewart & Co. By 1920, both had been rebuilt at Derby, which included a larger superheated boiler with Belpaire firebox. Although not readily apparent, at 7ft 0½ ins, the diameter of the driving wheels of these ex-Midland '2Ps', was 3½ ins larger than the later LM&S Class '2P' locomotives. They also differed with right-hand drive. It might also be noted that these two locomotives (as featured above and on page 80) had different style chimneys, No. 40505 having been given a replacement tall chimney of Stanier design.

In his book British Locomotives from the Footplate *(Ian Allan, 1950), author O.S. Nock, referred to the piloting work undertaken by the Class '2P' 4-4-0s, especially the (then) already elderly Midland Railway examples No's 505 and 509 still hard at work on the S&D, in the following terms: 'One thinks with amusement of that Derby Society for the Prevention of Cruelty to Engines, to which the late D.W. Sanford once alluded, when one of these old stalwarts comes thundering up past Chilcompton, double-heading the 'Pines Express', and going well-nigh 'all out' on full regulator and 55 per cent cut-off!' Those of us who can recall such sights and sounds at first hand know exactly what Mr Sandford meant, although no such 'all-out' efforts were required by the likes of No. 40505 when working the local S&D passenger traffic, as portrayed in Norman's picture above.*

Ivatt Class '4MT' 2-6-0 No. 43017 had been in service just four years when photographed here in charge of the 3.30pm Bristol (Temple Meads)-Bournemouth West on the climb south of Midsomer Norton. In their original double-chimney form, these locomotives were not good performers and the three allocated to the S&D were, apparently, considered only marginally better than the Class '2P' 4-4-0s. By the commencement of the 1953 summer services, all three had been transferred away from the line. *3rd June 1952*

This is the section of track which the Somerset & Dorset Railway Heritage Trust is currently (2008) planning to restore and reopen as they break out from their base at Midsomer Norton South station. In this view, the station lies beyond the bend round which the track disappears in the background.

No. 40509 emerges from Chilcompton Tunnel with the 4.37pm Bath – Templecombe. 3rd June 1952
Although this was the favourite viewpoint for photographers at this location, on those few occasions I paid a visit here in the early 1960s, I much preferred to cross the field to the lineside a little to the north of the tunnel where, as seen in some of Norman's photographs, the progress of a heavy Down train could be followed (and certainly heard) climbing the gradient all the way from just south of Midsomer Norton station as far as the approach into Chilcompton Tunnel.

SOME OLD FAVOURITES

More than three and a half years after Nationalisation of the railways, old S&D No. 59 still shows, on the side of her tender, evidence of a previous era. Now, however, the shed plate carried was the Southern Region code '71H' (Templecombe) and the Class '4F' 0-6-0 now bears the number 44559 as it heads the 3.10pm Bath-Templecombe through Lyncombe Vale on the climb towards Combe Down Tunnel. This mid-afternoon local was typical of the stopping trains on the S&D, calling at all stations and taking just short of two hours to complete the 37 mile journey to Templecombe. Providing you could spare the time, this was by far the best way to enjoy the passing delights of the Somerset countryside, once past the sulphurous passage of Devonshire and Combe Down Tunnels! *22nd August 1951*

Recalling Norman's photograph taken here in 1936 (see page 20), I commented in the caption therein how the many glasshouses to be seen then on the hillside above the line were destined to be replaced by some rather nice semi-detached houses, fronting Greenway Lane. Well, here they are – seen on the skyline in the photograph above. What a marvellous place for an S&D enthusiast to live – just imagine the view from the back garden!

When, later in the 1950s, Norman Lockett moved to live in Bath, he had only a half-mile walk to the lineside at Lyncombe Vale. Accordingly, this wonderful location, little more than a mile south of Bath city centre, became a favourite whenever he could be persuaded away from photographing the products of Swindon as viewed from the end of the platforms at Bath Spa station! Norman would have used the narrow and easily missed steeply sloping (and sometimes very slippery!) footpath leading down from Greenway Lane (here on the skyline) to cross over Devonshire Tunnel, just a little before the S&D line emerged into this almost hidden valley which, apparently, some visiting photographers had great difficulty in finding! In my own (much) younger days, a visit here was only taken as a diversion from a bicycle ride between Midford and Bath (usually on the return leg, having been ejected from the lineside opposite Green Park shed) which, although only a few miles in length, involved some very hard peddling and usually quite a bit of pushing the bike on foot. My two-wheeled steed was left, completely unattended, in Greenway Lane whilst I (and sometimes some school friends) descended on foot to observe the summer Saturday activities of the S&D in Lyncombe Vale for an hour or so. Never a second thought that the bicycle (or any part of it) would not still be there when I returned – how, sadly, times have changed!

Class '2P' 4-4-0 No. 40563 pulls away from Midford with a Bath to Templecombe train the details of which – most unusually – Norman failed to record. The lineside building was Midford 'B' Ground Frame and controlled the set of points serving the Up siding. As I recalled when first rambling on about Midford right back on page 10, the ground frame was interlocked with and released by a lever in Midford Signal Box, which can be seen in the left background, on the far side of the 168 yards long viaduct. Having just mentioned the delights of the Somerset countryside to be enjoyed through the carriage window of an S&D train, in my opinion, nowhere on the northern half of the line could it be bettered than between the southern end of Combe Down Tunnel and as far as Shoscombe. *Summer 1952*

This is another of those few photographs David has found where his father used film negative rather than a glass plate. David could also find no evidence that a print had ever been made. We debated with our publisher about that telegraph pole – we lost our argument, so in it remains! Come to think of it, the stay wires might have looked rather odd without also including the post to which they were attached.

FIRST SIGNS OF A NEW REGIME

Seen from the lane leading to Twinhoe, Class '4F' 0-6-0 No. 44096 crosses Midford Viaduct with the 5.0pm Bath to Evercreech Junction freight. *9th September 1953*

At first sight, the influence of the Western Region (under whose commercial management the northern half of the S&D was now controlled) appeared to have made no difference to the line but look carefully at this and the previous photograph, as both reveal examples of the changes which were starting to be made. In the previous view, Midford 'B' Ground Frame, the signal box and, beyond, the station buildings are still in the livery of the former Southern Railway. However, in the picture above, the Western Region painters have been in action and the ground frame, signal box and station buildings have all been repainted in the chocolate and cream house colours of the WR. At the same time, the canopy over the station platform (just visible in the previous photograph) was removed in order to avoid repair and future maintenance costs.

AFTERNOON LOCALS

The newly painted Midford 'B' Ground Frame and Up inner home signal feature as Class '4F' 0-6-0 No. 44102, built for the MR by Kerr Stuart, accelerates away gently from a first station stop and heads southwards towards Wellow with the 3.15pm Bath-Templecombe stopping train. During the 1950s, the 3.15pm from Bath continued to provide a good local connection from the Down 'Pines' which departed Green Park station just ten minutes earlier. *9th September 1953*

Ex-LM&S Class '2P' No. 40698 climbs the 1 in 60 gradient away from Midford with the 4.37pm Bath-Templecombe. This was another local service which provided a good connection from Bath, this time out of the 3.25pm (SX) Gloucester or 10.30am (SO) Liverpool to Bournemouth. During mid June to mid September, there was also a 10.38am (SO) Manchester-Bournemouth through train which departed Bath at 4.36pm. On such days, the departure of the 4.37pm local service was put back by ten minutes. Notice the milepost on the extreme right, signifying a distance of 4¼ miles as measured from the start of the S&D at Bath Junction. *9th September 1953*

JOINT EFFORT ON A JOINT LINE!

A combination of motive power which typified the 'Joint' nature of the S&D. Class '2P' 4-4-0 No. 40563 (the first of the class to be built, in 1928, during the regime of the LM&SR) and ex-SR 'West Country' Class 4-6-2 No. 34041 *Wilton* head the southbound 'Pines Express' across the three arch Watery Bottom Viaduct. On weekdays between early June and mid September 1953, the Down 'Pines' was scheduled to depart Bath at 3.05pm. Norman Lockett recorded the time of this photograph as 3.30pm, so here, on passing through Lyncombe Vale, the train was nearly twenty minutes down on schedule! Such delays did not, however, necessarily mean other than a 'right time' arrival at Bournemouth, providing the inevitable efforts to regain time were not thwarted by delays in the passing loops on the single line sections south of Templecombe or by traffic congestion approaching the end of the journey. *26th August 1953*

The SR Authorities had introduced their 'Light Pacifics' to the S&D in 1951, in anticipation that the tractive effort of these locomotives would enable ten coach trains to be run, unassisted, between Bath and Evercreech Junction. This would have eased considerably the need for double-heading. Unfortunately, the 'Green Goddesses' (as they were nicknamed) were found to be rather erratic performers over the line and their maximum permitted load over the Mendip Hills was fixed as equal to eight coaches, the same as the Stanier Class '5s'.

SECTION 4
1953 TO 1957
FIVE HALCYON YEARS FOR THE LINESIDE OBSERVER

To those enthusiasts who have memories of the S&D during the post-war era, the period from the early to the late 1950s represented, I suspect, the halcyon years. These were the last years when 'the masses' who, with the benefit of holidays with pay could now afford a week at the seaside, still relied on the railways to carry them to and from their annual holiday. Whilst petrol rationing had at last been withdrawn in late May 1950, it would still be some years – towards the end of the 1950s – before the level of general prosperity had risen to the extent whereby more and more people could consider the purchase of their own first car. Until those circumstances arose, each summer Saturday throughout much of the 1950s heralded a procession of through trains carrying large numbers of holidaymakers from the North of England and the Midlands, over the S&D on the last leg of their journeys to Bournemouth. In the opposite direction, those who had completed their week by the sea were carried northwards by an equally generous provision of trains. At that time of intense activity over the S&D, few enthusiasts could have guessed how soon before this pattern would change!

As holiday passenger traffic became ever heavier, the S&D lineside observer could witness the sight and sounds of the many double-headed trains doing battle with the gradients over the Mendip Hills and taking their turn to negotiate the single line sections. During the week, freight traffic continued to dominate, although the 1955 National Rail Strike proved one of those defining events that persuaded many commercial and industrial customers to transfer some or all of their custom to road transport as soon as was feasible.

Since February 1950, the motive power in use on the S&D had been under the control of the Southern Region, with most of the locomotives on loan from the LMR. In mid April 1953, the locomotive stock was formally transferred to the SR and this would remain the case until 1958. The regular use of the Bulleid 'Light Pacifics' over this difficult route from 1951 did not prove the success that had been hoped but, in 1954, the S&D received a first allocation of three brand new BR Standard Class '5' 4-6-0s, which immediately became firm favourites with the locomotive crews.

As the 1950s progressed, more and more examples of the BR 'Standards' saw use on the route, something which, by the end of the decade, served to change some of the unique atmosphere of the line, by heralding the decline of those classes of motive power more traditionally associated with the S&D.

Despite the introduction to the S&D of the Bulleid 'Light Pacifics' in 1951, two years later some of the Stanier Class '5' 4-6-0s, with their proven reliability, continued to see service over the line. One of these was No. 44839, seen here at Chilcompton Tunnel with the 3.30pm Bristol (Temple Meads)-Bournemouth. However, just four months later, this locomotive would be transferred away and reallocated from Bath to Derby. It has been recorded that the LMR authorities were calling for the return of at least some of their 'Fives' and, with some reluctance, No's 44826/30/39 were transferred from the S&D to 'pastures new' during the same week in September 1953. *26th May 1953*

MASBURY SUMMIT

Viewed from the overbridge (Bridge No. 69), large-boilered S&D Class '7F' No. 53806 approaches the summit of the line near Masbury with the 10.45am Midsomer Norton-Evercreech Junction coal train, assisted at the rear by one of Radstock's 'Jinty' Class '3F' 0-6-0 tank locomotives (it was a very hot day), both locomotives will have been working very hard. The train had climbed more than 300 feet since leaving Norton Hill Colliery, with a pause of ten minutes which allowed for the '7F' to take water at Chilcompton. This final section of the southbound climb was graded at 1 in 73. At Evercreech Junction, this freight would be shunted into the yard for inspection and, if necessary, reformed before proceeding southwards. Most likely this would be by means of one of the several weekday 'trip' workings to the Upper Yard at Templecombe. *25th May 1953*

This view, along with that opposite, at Masbury Summit, 811 feet above sea level and the highest point on the S&D, were both taken on a day of bright sunshine; very different to the conditions when the Mendips were enveloped in mist or fog, or even more dramatic, following a heavy fall of snow. Much of the climb in both directions was very exposed but the summit was located in a deep cutting. Much has been written about the southbound climb from Radstock whereas, overall, the ascent faced by northbound trains was, if anything, an even greater challenge. A favoured location for generations of photographers, Bridge. 69 carried the road from Oakhill to Green Ore and Cheddar over the line.

Turning to look southwards over the opposite parapet of Oakhill Road Bridge, Class '2P' 4-4-0 No. 40563 and a Stanier Class '5' 4-6-0 breast the summit with the northbound 'Pines Express'. All but the first two carriages of the train are still on the upgrade, the final approach to the summit in this direction being 1 in 50. This was followed by just 110 feet of level track before the commencement of the 7½ mile descent, all the way to Radstock. So although not readily apparent here, the leading locomotive had already reached the start of the downgrade. The assisting locomotive had obviously played its part, juging from the fact that the 'Black Five' had steam to spare. *25th May 1953*

Note the lengthman, no doubt walking his patch, along the cess on the Down side of the summit. When viewing scenes such as this, I sometimes wonder how the lineside cuttings and embankments might have looked today, had the S&D survived into the 21st Century. Certainly nowhere near the standard seen here, if the state of much of the rural railway network nowadays is any indicator!

'TI' EXCURSION

Early in 1954, Ian Allan Ltd, the publisher of the monthly magazine *Trains Illustrated,* organised a 'Somerset & Dorset Excursion'. As will be seen by comparing the advertisement *(next page)* with Norman Lockett's photograph, below, all did not go exactly to plan! The proposal to use an ex-L&SWR Class 'T9' 4-4-0 to assist a 'Schools' Class 4-4-0 over the S&D had to be abandoned because of problems fitting a tablet exchanger to the 'T9's tender for use along the single line sections of the route. So, almost at the last minute, none too clean Class '2P' 4-4-0 No. 40601 was provided to accompany No. 30932 *Blundell's,* for what was thought to be a unique visit of a 'Schools' class to the Somerset & Dorset. It was soon pointed out, however, that one of the same class had twice been seen in charge of a troop train over the S&D during the Second World War!

Having just emerged from Combe Down Tunnel, and, with No. 30932 *Blundell's* leading, the '*Trains Illustrated* Excursion' passes under Mogers Bridge (No. 13) on the 1 in 50 descent towards Devonshire Tunnel and Bath Junction. *25th April 1954*
Note: When this negative was located by David Lockett, the glass plate was found to be broken in two. Thankfully, with the aid of digital imaging software, the damage has been 'repaired' so that the break is (almost) invisible. Likewise there had been some deterioration in the bottom right corner of the glass plate, although this has been mostly cropped out here.

For the first leg of the return run, No. 40601 was accompanied by another Class '2P', No. 40698. The pair are seen here emerging from Chilcompton Tunnel and were subsequently recorded as having made a very spirited descent of the Mendips, with a maximum speed in excess of 60 mph. No. 30932, which could not be turned at Templecombe, ran back 'light engine' ahead of the special, was turned at Evercreech Junction and continued to Templecombe. There, the special was taken over again by the 'Schools' for the journey home to London via Salisbury and the SR main line to Waterloo. *25th April 1954*

"T1" RAILFAN EXCURSION
TO THE
SOMERSET & DORSET
SECTION
ON
SUNDAY, 25th APRIL, 1954

"BOURNEMOUTH LIMITED" TO RUN AGAIN

Headed by a "Schools" Class 4-4-0 this special will run at high speed from Waterloo to Bournemouth Central non-stop. Then the train will proceed over the arduous S. & D. section, with the "Schools" piloted by a "T9" 4-4-0 to Bath Green Park, where approximately 1½ hours is allowed. The train will then return to Templecombe (Upper) for a high-speed run back to Waterloo.

FARES: ADULT 28/-; JUVENILE 16/- inclusive

RESTAURANT CARS WILL RUN IN THE TRAIN for the service of light lunch and full dinner, bookable in advance, price 11s. inclusive and for light refreshments at standard prices.

BOOK NOW TO *Jan Allan Ltd.*
S. & D. EXCURSION

CRAVEN HOUSE
HAMPTON COURT
SURREY

CLOSURE OF A LITTLE KNOWN S&D OUTPOST

When David Lockett came across the previously unprinted glass plate negative of this scene, I knew immediately I had to find an 'excuse' to include it in these pages. It is the little-photographed former Midland Railway station at St Philips, Bristol and the link is that, for very many years, it served as an outpost to some of the services to and from the S&D. Sited on the north side of the adjacent goods yard and comprising only a single platform, the station opened on 2nd May 1870, having been provided to ease congestion at Temple Meads, which had been used by trains to and from the Midland station at Bath since services commenced on 4th August the previous year. This situation was eased from the early 1930s, following the modernisation and enlargement of Temple Meads, although St Philips continued to be used until closed from Sunday 21st September 1953. Norman Lockett took this single photograph on the Wednesday preceding closure, showing the station frontage as seen from the granite sett access which led down from Midland Road. The location had been very convenient for the shopping centre, as it existed before the heavy bomb damage suffered during World War 2. The station, which did not escape the ravages of the aerial bombardments, remained mostly unrepaired and unpainted, including the nameboard facing the forecourt. Norman recorded the time of his photograph as 5.15pm, so Ivatt 2-6-2 Class '2MT' No. 41242 (new to Bath in October 1949) will have worked the 4.30pm from Bath (Green Park) which was scheduled to arrive at 5.11pm. During that final summer, the public timetable showed a weekday (Mon. to Fri.) service of nine departures; one to Yate, the remainder to Green Park, one of which (the 6.00pm) still comprised through stock over the S&D to Bournemouth West. Arrivals also totalled nine, all from Bath, including the 3.35pm from Bournemouth, conveying a mails van which was detached at Mangotsfield and added to the 'Northern Postal'. No services used the station for the more than four hours between the 11.50am departure and the 4.14pm arrival! Saturday services differed little and no trains used the station on Sundays. After closure, all services were transferred to Temple Meads. *16th September 1953*

Bath to Bristol Temple Meads via the former Midland route was 14³/₄ miles (about a quarter mile less to St Philips) as compared with only 11¹/₄ miles via the former GWR main line. Average times for all stations locals were 38-40 mins and about 18 mins respectively. As far as I can recall, the fares in the 1950s were much the same, so true enthusiasts got more for their money 'via Mangotsfield'. At least, that was my excuse for trying to persuade a parent extremely reluctant to journey that way on an occasional visit from Trowbridge to Bristol. Doubtless, however, it was the walk between the two stations at Bath which really proved the deterrent!

For those wondering why I haven't mentioned the motor car, identification of it proved somewhat difficult; I didn't have a clue, I'm afraid – wrong sort of motive power! However, our publisher contacted motoring expert Malcolm Bobbitt, for his opinion as to what the vehicle might be:

'There are few clues to assist identification in this rear end view. It could well be a Morris or Humber but I'm worried about the rear-mounted spare wheel; those aforementioned models of the mid-1930s usually had sidemount spare wheels. Then there is the roof design, where in this instance the roof appears to be fabric covered. It could be that the car in question has a Weymann type body which would have had a fabric covering. The vehicle is obviously a luxury machine of some considerable size and I'm wondering if it might be a Rover or an Austin Sixteen/Eighteen. I have a feeling a positive identity is not going to be possible. If only we had more of a three-quarter rear view, which might have given greater detail about the body design.' All I can say is that its much easier with locomotives!

THE BR STANDARD CLASS '5' 4-6-0s COME TO THE S&D

During late May and early June 1954, the S&D received three brand new BR Standard Class '5' 4-6-0s, No's 73050-52. Almost immediately, they came to be acknowledged as just the locomotives needed to handle this most challenging of routes and, like the Stanier 'Black Fives' on which they were, in part, modelled, they became and remained firm favourites with the S&D footplate crews and the men who maintained them. Here, Standard Class '5' No. 73052 waits at Evercreech Junction with the 9.55am Bath to Bournemouth West. *11th October 1954*

We step back in time a few weeks, to the early summer of 1954, as ex-MR Class '2P' 4-4-0 No. 40509, by this date nearly sixty years old, assists BR Standard Class '5' 4-6-0 No. 73051, then less than two months old, with the southbound 'Pines Express'. Of the many of Norman's views featuring this, my personal favourite lineside location – the stone wall overlooking the S&D just to the south of Midford Viaduct – I selected this one which included the enthusiast, reminding me of the many hours I spent here and the realisation (somewhat later in life!) of just how lucky I had been to witness such scenes. *26th June 1954*

Just to give some idea of how the S&D followed the contours around the interlocking hillsides, draw, if you will, an imaginary line upwards from the chimney of No. 40509. On the farthest hillside you might just notice (a little to the right) a house. The southern exit from Combe Down Tunnel lay lower down that same hillside. The route described by the line ran towards the right of this view ((to a distant position out of sight behind the prominent lineside tree in the centre right foreground), before reversing direction to pass through the parklands of Midford Castle (hidden in the trees), then appearing into view to pass through Midford station and out onto the viaduct. The reverse curvature was very much a feature of this beautiful section of the line. Incidentally, the blurred wall in the foreground indicates Norman had pushed the depth of focus of his camera to the limit here but what a fabulous photograph nevertheless.

DEVONSHIRE BANK

Class '2P' 4-4-0 No. 40568 and one of Bath's allocation of 'West Country' 4-6-2s, No. 34041 *Wilton*, attack Devonshire Bank on the 1 in 50 climb out of Bath with the 'Pines Express'. This was a popular location for photographers (and trainspotters!) – a footbridge just 100 yards before the line entered the 440 yards Devonshire Tunnel. Note on the left the 'pre-fabs' erected at Moorfields by Bath City Council, to provide housing following the wartime damage to dwellings in and around the city. Built nationwide but intended only as a short-term facility, these dwellings proved extremely popular and some (although not those in Bath) have lasted into the 21st century. *1st September 1954*

Following the end of the summer service in 1954, the Bulleid 'Light Pacifics' based at Bath since 1951 were transferred away. However, as will be seen, examples of the same class based at Bournemouth shed continued to be rostered over the line regularly on busy summer Saturdays and, less frequently, during weekdays.

A little author's licence here, as we move forward in time but remain at the same location, looking in the opposite direction towards the tunnel and the bonus of a pair of Standard BR 'Fives' working in tandem! Although this picture comes from a later date, there is nothing in the view to suggest that this is the final summer of through traffic over the S&D, rather than the mid 1950s. Consecutively numbered 73051 and 73052 coast out of Devonshire Tunnel, making use of the gradient as they speed downhill towards Bath Junction with the 12 noon Bournemouth West to Huddersfield relief. *18th August 1962*

Returning to the mid 1950s, here we see the third member of Bath's allocation of brand new BR 'Fives'. On a glorious spring afternoon, with the trees and well manicured lineside hedgerows yet to break into leaf, the fresh air in Lyncombe Vale must have seemed even more welcome following the passage of Devonshire Tunnel (extreme left). Class '2P' 4-4-0 No. 40564 and BR Standard Class '5' 4-6-0 No. 73050 are in charge of the southbound 'Pines'. The small underbridge beneath the connection between the first and second coaches was known as Ketleys Bridge (No. 11). This was probably the name of the person who owned the nursery and glasshouses when the line was built, features which – as already mentioned – existed here, for many years. *20th April 1955*
No. 73050 arrived on the line in June 1954, some weeks after its two 'sisters', having been selected to be shown at the International Railway Congress Association Exhibition at Willesden. For that reason, it had been 'bulled up' with a special exhibition finish, in which superb condition it first appeared at Bath shed in June 1954.

TEMPLECOMBE 'TRANSFER'

ABOVE: Another of the former S&D Class '4F' 0-6-0s, No. 44558, heads south near Horsington with a freight which will terminate at Templecombe. Norman recorded the time as 12 noon, so this was probably the 11.35am 'trip' working from Evercreech Junction. A number of these workings were scheduled for each weekday in both directions, the sorting of wagons destined for (or received from) the former L&SWR line having been carried out in the yards at Evercreech Junction. The train is passing Templecombe No. 3 Junction intermediate Down home signal with its co-acting arms, located just over ¾ mile north of Templecombe Junction (formerly No. 2) Signal Box. Just visible in the distance is the lineside cottage at Cheriton Crossing. *9th October 1954*

OPPOSITE PAGE BOTTOM: It appears that Norman Lockett did not take a photograph depicting an S&D train at the main line station at Templecombe. However, just to give a flavour of the station, which many referred to as Templecombe Upper, this is a main line service featuring 'Merchant Navy' Class 'Pacific' No. 35008 *Orient Line* heading eastwards through platform 2. The awning which can be seen on the extreme right covered part of the platform used by S&D trains. The extensive sidings for the exchange of freight traffic between the two systems lay just to the rear of the train, on the Up side of the main line. *8th September 1957*

ABOVE: Having climbed the 1 in 100 spur from Templecombe No. 2 Junction, Class '2P' 4-4-0 No. 40696 approaches Platform 3 at the Upper station to conclude what would have been a leisurely run down the line with the 1.10pm stopping train from Bath. Note the water tank to the Up side of the line leading towards No. 2 Junction, often used by freight traffic and light engines whilst waiting pilot duties between the S&D line and Upper station. *9th October 1954*

THE VERSATILE CLASS '4F' 0-6-0s

Returning, briefly, to the start of the 1950s, this view depicts a '4F' doing the type of work for which the class had actually been designed, although this lightweight load of vans forming the 5.0pm freight from Bath would not have proved any challenge to No. 44560 on the climb towards Chilcompton. It may also explain why, on this occasion, the train was recorded running half-an-hour ahead of schedule. *19th July 1950*
The performance of these locomotives over the S&D has sometimes been belittled in more recent years. However, despite some undisputed shortcomings, the Class '4F' 0-6-0s continued to be employed for a variety of services on the S&D for very many years, proving how useful they were even when allocated tasks which must have been beyond the primary intentions of their designer!

The extremely picturesque Midford Valley looks at its best on a glorious summer afternoon as No's 44102 and 44559 attack the 1 in 60 grade around the reverse curves south of Midford station. The train is the 10.38am (SO) Manchester to Bournemouth, a service to which a pair of '4Fs' were rostered over the S&D on a regular basis during much of the early 1950s. *26th June 1954*
No. 44102 was one of the first batch of the LM&S Class '4F' 0-6-0s built at Stoke-on-Trent by Kerr Stuart & Co. No. 44559 was constructed by Armstrong, Whitworth & Co. for the S&DJR (as No. 59) in 1922.

No. 44558 approaches Shepton Mallet (Charlton Road) station with the 9.03am Bristol-Bournemouth service. Behind the train can be seen Charlton Road Viaduct (No. 84) which, comprising 27 arches and a length of 307 yards, was the biggest on the S&D. In the background (behind the large CWS factory), the Mendip Hills rise towards Masbury, illustrating just how much the S&D had to climb to reach the summit of the line. The sidings on the right once served the headquarters of the Somerset & Dorset Signalling Department. *29th September 1956*

Was this a 'piece of luck' for Norman or a very carefully timed shot? A split second earlier release of the shutter would have resulted in that lofty lattice post, carrying the Up starting signal, appearing to emerge straight out of the chimney of No. 44558!

SOME ELDERLY MOTIVE POWER

ABOVE: **Johnson Class '3F' 0-6-0 No. 43216 passes Horsington and nears the end of its journey with the 2.20pm Highbridge-Templecombe service. As related earlier, this locomotive had begun its working life as S&DJR No. 72, when delivered new from Neilson Reid & Co. of Glasgow in 1902. At the start of the 1950s, there were seven or eight of these 0-6-0s still in service on the S&D and No. 43216 was destined to be the last withdrawn in 1962.** *29th September 1956*

OPPOSITE PAGE TOP: **It might be argued that ex-MR Class '2P' 4-4-0 No. 40509 was not as elderly, because although dating from 1899, this locomotive had been substantially rebuilt (as one of the '483' Class) by the Midland Railway at Derby in 1912! Seen here approaching Winsor Hill Tunnel with 12.55pm Bournemouth West-Bath, this proved to be Norman Lockett's last photograph of the locomotive, which was to be withdrawn from service in June 1957. Sister engine No. 40505 had been set aside in October 1953, whilst No. 40527, paradoxically, another ex-MR member of the class and which was transferred from Chester Northgate as a replacement, lasted only until early 1956.** *11th October 1954*

OPPOSITE PAGE BOTTOM: **Also nearing the end of her days, Johnson 0-4-4T Class '1P' No. 58051 climbs around the curve leading to Templecombe SR station with the 2.20pm from Highbridge. Built at Derby in 1886, this locomotive had transferred to Highbridge during the summer of 1952, as a replacement for No. 58047. Apparently, the Belpaire boiler shown here was only fitted at Derby at the start of 1952. No. 58051 was withdrawn in October 1956, by which date it was the last survivor of the class to have been built at Derby, the few members still then remaining having been built by Dübs & Co.** *9th October 1954*

Although jumping ahead a little in time, this would appear to be an appropriate place to include this final shot of Johnson 0-4-4T No. 58086, which became the last of this once-numerous class to remain in service anywhere in the country. Having only recently been set aside when photographed here on 16th May 1959, No. 58086 remained at Bath shed until finally towed away for scrapping in early September 1960. Note the shedplate had already been removed. Forty-seven years later, the shedplate, together with the smokebox numberplate and a worksplate, came into the ownership of the S&DR Trust. They are all held in the Trust's museum at Washford, on the West Somerset Railway.

Behind No. 58086, one is left in no doubt that here stood part of the large industrial complex of Stothert & Pitt, the world renowned manufacturers of cranes – quite a stark contrast to the Georgian architecture of the Lansdown area of the city, which forms the distant backdrop to this view.

THE POPULAR IVATT TANKS

No. 41248 emerges from Combe Down Tunnel into the sunshine in Horsecombe Vale with the 4.35pm Bath to Templecombe train. The train comprises one of the Maunsell 3-sets (390-9) all built at Eastleigh in 1926. The crimson and cream livery was applied to this stock between 1950 and 1956, and all were withdrawn by September 1961. *20th April 1955*

Four of the Ivatt Class '2MT' 2-6-2Ts, No's 41240-43, were allocated new to Bath in October 1949. Primarily, they were intended as replacements for the 0-4-4Ts employed on the services over the former Midland line between Bath and Bristol, on which they proved a great success. Within a few months following arrival at Bath, No. 41241 was seen from March 1950, on a number of dates, on the Templecombe, Evercreech Junction and Burnham branch line services. Far more dramatic, Ivo Peters recorded No. 41240 assisting an Up relief train on 26th August 1950, although whether this was a trial or (more likely) born out of desperation on a very busy summer Saturday will never be known! Whatever the reason, Ivo reported that word came down from on high that it should never be repeated. To the best of my own recollections, the Ivatt tanks were never widely seen on the S&D main line north of Evercreech Junction, other than when given an occasional evening run out with the 'Six-Five-Special'(those of you with memories of the BBC rock'n'roll programme will recall the significance) – the 6.05pm Bath to Binegar and return.

No. 41248, built at Crewe during the third quarter of 1948, together with No. 41249, were later additions to the S&D allocation when transferred in the summer of 1953 to Templecombe. On the S&D, the Ivatt's main domain became 'the branch' and workings from Templecombe over the 'Dorset' end of the main line, including the Bailey Gate 'Milky'. Always a popular design, locomotives of this class retained a lasting association with the S&D right up until closure in 1966. Indeed, as we shall later see, they were very much in evidence on the sad final weekend.

In early June 1956, the S&D received an allocation of three BR Standard Class '4' 4-6-0s, No's 75071-73, transferred from Exmouth Junction. Norman Lockett returned to a favourite lineside location, south of Midsomer Norton, to capture his first picture of one of this trio. No. 75073, built at Swindon in 1953, climbs with the 3.25pm Gloucester-Bournemouth semi-fast towards Chilcompton Tunnel. Gradually, as the allocation of these locomotives increased (there were eight by 1961), they would take over many of the tasks previously performed by the Class '2P' 4-4-0s. *7th August 1956*

RIGHT: To conclude this section, we return to the first half of the 1950s, with photographs which represent the S&D just before the arrival of the first allocations of the BR Standard types of motive power. Chilcompton Tunnel is the location of this combination, which could only be seen on the S&D! Class '2P' 4-4-0 No. 40563 assists Bulleid 4-6-2 No. 34040 *Crewkerne* as they climb hard up the 1 in 53 gradient with the southbound 'Pines'. The 'West Country' still retained most of its original features, including the 'as built' cab front. *15th July 1953*

NEW AND ESTABLISHED MOTIVE POWER

BELOW: Hardly a taxing load, this six-coach train was well within the limits of a Stanier 'Black Five'. No. 44917, transferred to Bath the previous year, bowls up towards Masbury Summit in charge of the 9.05am Bristol Temple Meads-Bournemouth West. The driver, leaning from his cabside window, was no doubt enjoying the passing scenery which, on such a sunny early summer morning, was at its best. *25th May 1953*

A photograph to prove that, just occasionally, Norman reached the southern end of the line or, to be more accurate, beyond the southern extremity of the S&D (at Broadstone), as this location lies on that section of the former L&SWR route used by S&D services to reach Poole and Bournemouth. Running six minutes late with the 6.05am Bristol-Bournemouth stopper, ex-LM&S Class '2P' 4-4-0 No. 40697 pulls away from Parkstone station and recommences the climb of Parkstone Bank, the 'sting in the tail' for southbound S&D trains. The worst of the climb, mostly at 1 in 60 to this point, will soon be over but there will be the better part of another mile to reach the summit at Branksome. There the train will diverge from the Southern main line to reach Bournemouth West station. The bridge in the background crosses the line immediately to the east of Parkstone station, for the passage of which the gradient was eased to 1 in 330, reverting immediately to 1 in 60. The change of gradient can be clearly seen. *24th June 1953*

SECTION 4
1958–1962
A HIDDEN AGENDA?

At first sight, all looked very much as before in this view taken at Bath shed early in 1958. Class '2P' 4-4-0 No. 40700 had been spruced up and sat out of steam in front of an S&D Class '7F' 2-8-0. However, although only four weeks had passed since control of the motive power transferred to the Western Region, No. 40700 already displayed an '82F' shed plate on its smokebox door. The circular concrete base in the foreground provided evidence of the large tank built in 1947 for the storage of oil, demolished after the locomotive oil-firing scheme was abandoned the following year. A good reserve of coal can be seen behind the Class '2P', whilst the buildings beyond are again part of the works of Messrs Stothert & Pitt. *3rd March 1958*

In retrospect, 1958 represented the 'watershed' in the post-war fortunes of the S&D. On 1st February 1958, British Railways implemented an adjustment to the regional boundary between those parts of the S&D administered by the Western Region and by the Southern Region. The boundary which had existed since 1950, at Cole, was moved to just south of Templecombe, excluding only the main line station at Templecombe which remained in Southern Region control. So, despite what appeared at first sight as a fairly minor change, not only did the WR now control the major part of the Somerset & Dorset but, other than the small engine shed at Branksome, all of the S&D motive power depots had become the responsibility of the Western.

The first outward signs of change came with the transfer of the motive power stock. The locomotives, which had displayed shed plates from the '71' group since 1950, now began to appear with plates numbered in the '82' (Bristol) group. The new allocations were '82F' for Bath (together with sub-sheds at Radstock and Highbridge), and '82G' for Templecombe.

In May 1958, the Working Timetable (WTT) for the services effective from 9th June was circulated to the appropriate personnel. For the first time, a Somerset & Dorset WTT carried the names of both the Southern and Western regions. It would prove to be the last

bespoke S&D WTT and the last time the entire length of the line appeared in one publication. Traditions were changing!

On the locomotive front, by late June 1958, the last two Stanier 'Black Fives' remaining at Bath were transferred back to the LMR, their places taken by additional BR Class '5' 4-6-0s. In November 1959, the first of the S&D Class '7F' 2-8-0s, No. 53800, was withdrawn. At the end of the year, the WR undertook some trials on the line with motive power of GWR origin. As the result, a number of the '22xx' Class 0-6-0s and a few 0-6-0 pannier tanks began to appear and – in the minds of many – they looked totally out of character on a line having such a long association with locomotives of Midland and LM&S origins.

During 1956, Norman Lockett first met Ivo Peters, when they both turned up to photograph the same train at Bath Spa station. The following year, Norman moved job and his family home to Bath. That may explain why, in 1957, he appears to have taken no photographs on the S&D! By 1958, he and Ivo Peters had become firm friends and, as such, they often visited the lineside together, sometimes standing 'shoulder to shoulder' to photograph the same scene. This, to some extent, has influenced the pictures we have selected to include in the remainder of this book, not wishing to replicate any more than necessary, similar pictures published previously by Ivo.

The southbound 'Pines Express' approaches Masbury Summit behind Class '2P' 4-4-0 No. 40568, assisting one of Bath's allocation of Standard Class '5' 4-6-0s. According to the time recorded by Norman, the train was running late, so possibly a spirited ascent from Radstock had been made with this heavy eleven coach loading. The fireman of the Class '5' has the injector on, no doubt replenishing the boiler now that the end of long climb is in sight. This would ensure there was adequate water cover before the locomotive tipped its nose over the summit and commenced the descent towards Shepton Mallet. Note the Ayrshire cattle, seemingly quite undisturbed by the passing train. *23rd August 1958*

The last two of Bath's allocation of Stanier Class '5' 4-6-0s were finally transferred back to the LMR in June 1958 but that did not bring to an end the appearance of 'Black Fives' over the S&D. This combination, climbing towards Combe Down Tunnel, was not a regular sight even by S&D standards! Class '7F' 2-8-0 No. 53808 assists the 4-6-0, which at this date must have been 'borrowed' for a return journey over the line. The train was the 2.45pm Bournemouth-Bristol and such an abundance of motive power for an eight-coach loading suggests either the Class '5' was not in good health or, more likely, the 2-8-0 had been coupled ahead to save a separate light engine path on a busy summer Saturday. Certainly, the train was benefiting from the double-heading; at the time recorded by Norman, the Working Timetable indicated the train should have only been passing Radstock, some 6 miles to the south! *23rd August 1958*

BORROWED 'BLACK FIVES'

Stanier Class '5' No. 45280, allocated to Saltley shed, had been noted earlier the same day in charge of a southbound special at Spetchley, on the former Midland main line from Birmingham to Bristol and Bath. Obviously too good an opportunity to miss, this was another case of a locomotive having been utilised by the Bath shedmaster for a return trip over the Mendips, before allowing it to head back towards Birmingham! Here, No. 45280 climbs away from Midford with the 3.35pm Bristol-Bournemouth. Departing Bath Green Park at 4.21pm, this was the service which, in earlier years had – as previously has been noted – commenced at Gloucester during the summer months, a practice which ceased at the end of the 1956 season. *16th May 1959*

In June 1959, No. 53800, the doyen of the original 1914 series of the S&D Class '7F' 2-8-0s, was sent to Derby, supposedly for overhaul. Apparently, however, such was the condition of the frames that the decision was taken to withdraw the locomotive and No. 53800 was cut up in January 1960. Here, some years earlier, on the last occasion Norman photographed the locomotive, the '7F' emerges from Chilcompton Tunnel running early with the 4.05pm Midsomer Norton to Evercreech coal train. This was a train which, when traffic demanded, could be started back at Radstock at 3.55pm, in which case departure from Midsomer Norton (having collected coal wagons from Norton Hill Colliery) would be retimed to 4.30pm. Notice how, over the years, it had been necessary to repair much of the original stone facing to the tunnel portal and wing walls. These repairs were undertaken in brick, the material originally used to form the arches. *11th May 1955*

I see we have reached page 114 of this tome without a mention of the engine head codes used on the S&D! The extract, below, is taken from the 1933 S&D Appendix to the Working Time Tables. The S&D's own head codes had survived not only the Grouping of the railways in 1923 but continued in use into the BR era and up until closure of the line in 1966. In 1958, upon the Western Region gaining full operational control of motive power matters, instructions were issued to conform to the standard engine head codes as used elsewhere. Typical of the S&D, this edict was only partially adopted for a few weeks, after which it was conveniently overlooked. As Midford signalman, Charlie Eyre, later told me, "Few out in the sticks on the S&D had a clue what the standard BR codes meant, so we just went back to using our own." Somehow, I suspect there may have been an element of fact in this!

ENGINE HEAD LAMPS.

Engines of S. & D. trains must carry head lamps as shown below:—

Engines of passenger trains	A white light at the foot of the chimney and a white light over the left-hand buffer.
Engines of freight trains	A white light at the foot of the chimney and a white light over the right-hand buffer.
Light engines	A white light at the foot of the chimney.

The lamps must be carried in position day and night.

When a train running on the S. & D. Joint Line is worked by two engines attached in front of the train, the second engine must not carry head lamps.

Class '4F' 0-6-0 No. 44559 and Class '7F' 2-8-0 No. 53807 are about to pass over the level crossing at the south end of Evercreech Junction station, with a train comprising twenty-one bogies which had been used earlier the same day to transport homing pigeons from the Midlands to Templecombe. Following liberation of the birds in the Lower Yard, the empty stock was worked back northwards. The train halted here at 'the Junction', to enable the Class '7F' to be turned before proceeding to Bath, where a pair of ex-GWR 'Moguls' were waiting to return the stock towards the Midlands. *16th May 1959*

Norman Lockett took this photograph by leaning over the palings at the side of the level crossing. The long shadow running across the track and up the side of the p-way trolley was cast by a very tall telegraph pole at the side of the A371 road. We were tempted to trim out this part of the photograph but this would have deprived you of that distant view of the countryside and, much nearer to hand, the pw trolley trailer!

Carrying reporting number '245', denoting the 7.47am Bradford (Forster Square)-Bournemouth working, Class '2P' 4-4-0 No. 40564 assists a BR Class '5' 4-6-0 southwards through the wayside station at Cole. Norman was standing on overbridge No. 121, Pitcombe Road Bridge, to obtain this view. In the left background, the five arch Cole Viaduct can be seen, whilst on the right is the former Railway Hotel. Very unusually, Norman omitted to record the exact date of this 1958 view. Note the haymaking season has started in the field to the side of the Up line.

BUSY BR 'FIVES'

BR Class '5' 4-6-0 No. 73019 speeds along the Stour Valley near Stourpaine & Durweston with the 3.40pm Bournemouth West-Bristol. Descending the grades from Blandford Forum, the single line extended for 16 miles all the way to Templecome No. 2 Junction. The first block section northwards from Blandford, along which No. 73019 is seen travelling, extended to Shillingstone, although in an earlier era of the line, this 5½ mile section could be divided, at busy times, by a passing loop situated just north of Stourpaine & Durweston Halt. *30th March 1959*

Like the Midford and Wellow valleys at the northern end of the S&D, the countryside through the Stour Valley was amongst the most picturesque on the route of the line. It is, however, quite different in character, being hereabouts a wider open valley as against the series of interlocking hills through which the S&D wound its way just to the south of Bath. This, of course, was long acknowledged as one of the delights of the S&D; the constantly changing countryside through which the railway passed.

The Down 'Pines Express' sets off from Bath Green Park behind Class '2P' 4-4-0 No. 40563 and an unidentified BR Class '5' 4-6-0. On the right is Bath Station Signal Box and just visible beyond is the Down starter for departures from the south platform (which the 'Pines' used), together with the Bath Junction Down distant for the S&D line. Notice the catcher extended from the front corner of the tender of the 4-6-0, ready to collect a pouch containing the tablet at Bath Junction for the single line to Midford. In the left background, the front of the S&D motive power shed can also be seen, whilst on the extreme right, part of the large Midland Bridge Road Goods Depot is visible. *3rd May 1958*

Just a few yards from where Norman took this photograph, the line crossed Victoria Bridge Road. At the side of the underbridge, at pavement level, there was a doorway in the retaining wall. This gave access to a flight of steps leading up to the lineside and a wonderful vantage place for 'locospotters' to observe all traffic, including movements on and off the shed. How long such pleasures lasted depended on whether or not we were all kicked out by a member of staff (which was most often the case) but that didn't stop many further such ventures!

No. 44560, another of the former S&DJR 'Armstrongs', sets off from a station stop at Midford with the 4.35pm Bath-Templecombe. The ropes seen knotted to the lower rail of the cattle truck behind the tender of the '4F' were, I suspect, used to tether any occupants. If so, the livestock were either too short to enjoy the view or had decided to keep their heads down! The rodding run at the near (Up) side of the ballast connected with lever 11 in Midford Signal Box, which was required to be pulled to release Midford 'B' Ground Frame. Whilst the Class '4F' 0-6-0s may not have been universally liked, they were reliable workhorses which continued to provide a variety of services on the S&D, as seen in this and the following two pictures. *3rd May 1958*

After many years of photographing trains from the side of the ballast at this location, Norman, on this occasion, climbed part-way up the side of the cutting leading to Chilcompton Tunnel! The 'Pines' is loaded to ten coaches, so 'West Country' Class 4-6-2 No. 34040 *Crewkerne* required the assistance of No. 44422, a Class '4F' built by the LM&S at Derby and first entering service in October 1927. *16th August 1958*

RIGHT: Templecombe based No. 44417, also constructed at Derby in 1927, breasts the summit of the single line on the climb from Corfe Mullen Junction and commences the descent to join the former L&SWR line at Broadstone. The train is the 12.23pm Templecombe-Bournemouth West and the triple-arch overbridge through which it is passing, No. 238, Ashington Lane Bridge, was one of the highest on the S&D. *3rd October 1954*

BELOW: There were at least a couple of occasions during June 1959 when a Bulleid 'Light Pacific' piloted the Down 'Pines Express'. Here, No. 34040 *Crewkerne*, together with BR Class '5' 4-6-0 No. 73051, regain double track at Midford on a glorious Saturday afternoon – the sort of day which made watching the passing trains from this location an absolute delight. No. 34040 was carrying a reporting number (M222) details of which the author has not been able to trace. It is suspected, however, that the number referred to a northbound relief working earlier in the day. If so, perhaps this had been an unbalanced working, which resulted in the locomotive being attached to the Down 'Pines' as a means of avoiding a separate light engine movement. *20th June 1959*

BR Class '5' 4-6-0 No. 73028 attacks the long curved 1 in 50 climb from Bath Junction with the 9.30am (Sundays) Bath-Bournemouth. This was always a popular summer service, calling at most of the more important intermediate locations, to arrive at Bournemouth just a couple of minutes before mid-day; the return journey commenced at 7.03pm. The 'BR5' is a ¼ mile into the climb and about to cross the ex-GW main line, with Bellotts Road visible on the right. This must have been one of the earliest runs over the S&D of No. 73028 which, together with No. 73019, had been transferred to Bath from Bristol (St Philips Marsh) in June 1958. Both arrived as replacements for the last two 'Black Fives' which had been returned to the LMR. *15th June 1958*

Running a few minutes late, Class '2P' 4-4-0 No. 40568 and a BR Standard Class '5' 4-6-0 attack the 1 in 50 gradient of Devonshire Bank in fine style as they lift the southbound 'Pines Express' out of Bath. Norman Lockett was obviously sufficiently pleased with this shot to include it in a folio of his photographs to be circulated that year, for comment amongst his contemporaries in the Railway Photographic Society. *26th April 1958*

AROUND COLE

One of Bath's allocation of BR Class '4' 4-6-0s, No. 75072, heads across Cole Viaduct with the 2.45pm (SO) Bournemouth-Bristol, the driver waving his arm to ackowledge the presence of the photographer. It looks as though two additional coaches had been added at the rear of this semi-fast service, which was recorded by Norman running 'right time'. This was another popular lineside location as, immediately to the north and just out of camera to the left of this view, the S&D crossed over the WR West of England main line, about a mile south of Bruton. *29th August 1959*
It was the section of line southwards from Cole station (which can just be seen here in the gap between the trees on the right) as far as Templecombe which had been transferred from Southern to Western Region control the previous year. Although, on the face of things, a minor length of the S&D route (totalling less than eight miles), it was significant in placing into WR hands a part of the line which included the motive power depot at Templecombe and, with it, the decision to transfer all S&D motive power to the Western Region.

Class '2P' 4-4-0 No. 40700 sets off from Cole with the 4.13pm Evercreech Junction to Templecombe. This was the service timed to provide a good connection from the Down 'Pines Express' at Evercreech Junction and which, on Saturdays only, continued southwards from Templecombe at 5.20pm, calling at all stations and halts as far as Broadstone, then only Poole and Bournemouth. Departure from Cole, the first station south of Evercreech Junction was scheduled for 4.20pm, which is exactly the time recorded here by Norman Lockett. The Up train standing in the station platform was the 4.05pm Templecombe to Evercreech Junction, which then formed the 5pm branch line train to Highbridge. *29th August 1959*

The Up line is already in the shadow cast by the side of the cutting as Johnson Class '3F' 0-6-0 No. 43194 ambles away from Cole with the 4.00pm from Highbridge. On summer Saturdays only, this train continued beyond Evercreech Junction as the 5.10pm to Templecombe, which is the service seen here. Cole station building can be seen through the Up line portal of Bridge No. 121. *29th August 1959*
I wonder whether Norman had arranged a lift to Cole in the car seen by the roadside to the left of the bridge and, if so, with whom, as the person seen here is not Ivo?

ABOVE: No. 73087 passes Midford goods yard on the single line section between Tucking Mill Viaduct and Midford station. The train is the 9.30am (Sundays only) Bath to Bournemouth, a service we last saw on another occasion climbing the bank out of Bath. This BR Class '5' 4-6-0 was allocated from the SR to Bath, for the summer months only, each year from 1956 to 1961. *16th August 1959*

I could never understand why the rail entrance to Midford goods yard was gated and the yard separated from the running line by a fence. I cannot recall any similar arrangement on the S&D other, of course, than where the sidings were in private ownership. The siding points and gate lock were controlled from a ground frame housed in a lineside hut – 'Midford A' – located just out of view to the left of this picture. The ground frame was released by the Bath Junction-Midford single line tablet. Both the ground frame and the siding connection were removed in June 1964. Notice the goods yard crane, provided to replace the original model in the early 1950s, and also the goods shed, which resembled more a traditional Dutch barn!

One had to be up early in order to observe the goods yard being shunted at Midford. The only service (at least during the era when I visited the line) to call here was the 5.50am goods train from Bath. Any traffic for the siding originating south of Midford was taken through to Bath and returned on the 5.50am the following day. Likewise, those few wagons or vans taken out of the yard and destined for the north of Midford, were first carried southwards by the 5.50pm as far as Radstock, there to be transferred to an Up service.

SR 'West Country' 'Light Pacific' No. 34041 *Wilton* sweeps up the start of the 1 in 60 climb away from Midford with the Down 'Pines' relief. Notice, in the left foreground, the former Up siding and the Midford 'B' Ground Frame had been removed. Used only *very* occasionally (usually only for traffic or engineering purposes), the siding was taken out of use by the latter part of 1959. *4th June 1960*

MORE
AROUND
MIDFORD

Summer 1959 had witnessed the first working over the S&D of a modified Bulleid 'Light Pacific', after which their use became a fairly regular occurrence, especially on summer Saturday through trains. Here, a year later, the 'Pines Express' crosses Midford Viaduct behind Class '2P' No. 40563 and 'West Country' No. 34045 *Ottery St Mary*. Note, by the way, the reporting number carried on the front of the 4-4-0. In 1960, a new system of four-character train identification was introduced by BR. The first digit identified the class of the train and the second the destination area (*e.g.* 'O' for a destination in the Southern Region), whilst the last two digits identified the individual train. During 1960, only some of the services over the S&D appeared with the new numbering but here is one example, the Down 'Pines' becoming train No. 1O95. *3rd September 1960*

One of the **BR Standard** types to be seen on the S&D was the Class '4' 2-6-0. None were ever allocated to the line but, from the spring of 1955, they became regular performers. They generally came from Eastleigh shed (71A), as was the case with No. 76015, which appears in this and the view lower opposite. Here, the engine is seen heading away southwards from Templecombe and about to pass under Bridge No. 155, which carried a minor road from Templecombe towards Buckhorn Weston, hauling the 9.05am Bristol (Temple Meads)–Bournemouth West. The SR main line, beneath which the S&D single line from Templecombe Junction passed, can be seen on the embankment in front of the houses in the background. *28th June 1958*

Bath shed had received three of the BR Standard Class '4' 4-6-0s, No's 75071-73, in June 1956. Here, the last of this original allocation heads past the tree-lined avenue near Wyke Campflower, about a mile to the north of Cole, with the 3.40pm Bournemouth-Bristol. *29th August 1959*
This was another particularly attractive stretch of the S&D and one of special significance. Look carefully, just to the right of the rear of the train and, almost hidden by the trees, you can just pick out the painted end of a lineside cottage. That, near enough, was the point where it is generally accepted that, in 1862, the Somerset Central Railway linked, head on, with the Dorset Central and so created the Somerset & Dorset Railway.

BR CLASS '4' 2-6-0S AND 4-6-0S

No. 76015 assists BR Class '5' No. 73050 through Midsomer Norton South, with a heavily laden Whit Sunday Bristol-Bournemouth excursion. *5th June 1960*
This was another wonderful location to observe the heavy southbound traffic, two miles into the climb from Radstock, as well as the shunting of empties and removal of loaded coal from nearby Norton Hill Colliery. Rail access to the colliery was gained immediately to the north of the underbridge sited at that end of the station.

S&D Class '7F' No. 53801 stands in the Down platform at Evercreech Junction on a lovely sunny evening in late August. Note the lengthening shadow of a telegraph pole falling across the smokebox of the locomotive! Other than the date and time, Norman gave no further details but, judging by those water cans placed on the front of the running plate, I suspect the 2-8-0, having just taken on water from the adjacent column, is about to set off, tender-first, towards Templecombe. In the distance, the Down advanced starting signal has already been pulled off, whilst just beyond the platform end, the level crossing gates have been closed across the road. The very tall Down starting signal, with its lower co-acting arm, is yet to be cleared. If I am correct in my assumption, then on the way towards Templecombe, a stop would be made at Bruton Road Crossing, less than one mile to the south, to put off the water cans for the crossing keeper's cottage, which had no mains supply. *29th August 1959*

TEST RUN WITH A 'NINE'

On a day of strong winds and incessant rain, driver Bill Rawles attends to the water supply from the lineside column at Evercreech whilst fireman Ron Bean stands aloft, ready to remove the 'bag' from the tender of BR Standard Class '9F' 2-10-0 No. 92204, on a test run from Bath to Bournemouth and back. Visible through the rain is a Class '2P' 4-4-0, standing in the middle road waiting to assist the Up 'Pines Express', due in about 25 minutes time. The purpose of the trial with the '9F' was to assess the suitability of the class for the S&D line, especially the ability to haul the 'Pines' and the summer Saturday holiday trains unassisted between Bath and Evercreech Junction, thus reducing the costly double-heading over the northern section. *29th March 1960*

Five hours later, No. 92204, with whistle blowing, makes a triumphant conquest of the Mendips, breasting Masbury Summit with the return test run to Bath. Despite the appalling weather, the trial – with an eleven coach train weighing 350 tons – was a complete success leading, just a few months later, to the allocation of four of the 2-10-0s to Bath for the duration of the summer season. *29th March 1960*

THE ARRIVAL OF THE '9F's

Following the successful trial of No. 92204 in March 1960, the '9F', along with classmates No's 92203/5/6, were allocated to Bath shed for the summer period. Norman appears to have photographed all bar No. 92206 during his visits to the lineside. Here, No. 92203, with a Walsall-Bournemouth August Bank Holiday excursion, sweeps up the long curving gradient which carried the line from the Stour Valley to the summit at Milldown, before reaching Blandford Forum. *1st August 1960*

On withdrawal, No. 92203 was purchased direct from BR by renowned wildlife conservationist and artist, David Shepherd, and taken first to the Longmoor Military Railway in Hampshire. The locomotive moved on to spend many years based at Cranmore on the East Somerset Railway, where David Shepherd named it Black Prince. In 1984, whilst working on the first of the 'Evercreech Junction' programmes filmed for BBC Bristol, I had the great pleasure of an afternoon on the footplate with ex-S&D footplate team Donald Beale and Peter Smith, and in the company of other former S&D railwaymen. At the time of writing, Black Prince is based at the Gloucestershire Warwickshire Railway, at Toddington.

No. 92204 regains double track after crossing Midford Viaduct with the 9.35am (SO) Sheffield-Bournemouth. *30th July 1960*

The driver acknowledges Norman with a wave as No. 92205 approaches the summit of the climb from Radstock with the 9.30am (Sundays) Bath-Bournemouth, the loading of which was of no challenge to a 'Nine'. *14th August 1960*

ENTHUSIAST'S SPECIALS

This must have been the first 'Ian Allan' enthusiast's special to visit the S&D since 1954. Ex-GWR 2-6-0 No. 6384 approaches Bath with the 'Severn & Wessex Express'. Having travelled from Paddington to Severn Tunnel Junction (where the 'Mogul' took over), the train then ran via the Severn Bridge and the former Midland main line to Mangotsfield and Bath. These Churchward 2-6-0s were not authorised to run over the S&D, the commencement of which can be seen bearing off left immediately this side of Bath Junction Signal Box, level with the rear of the train. *14th May 1960*

Prominent along the north side of the line, are the works of the former Bath Gas, Light & Coal Company, who were one of the first customers (possibly even the very first) of the Midland Railway when the line from Mangotsfield to Bath was opened in 1869. Coal continued to be brought in by rail until the introduction of North Sea gas, which heralded the end of gas production at the works, by this time part of South West Gas, in May 1971, some 5¼ years after passenger services had ceased to run. However, although consequently much reduced in size, the larger gasometers remained in use to store North Sea gas.

For the continuation of the run over the S&D, the 'Severn & Wessex Express' was hauled by No. 53807, seen here at Radstock, at the commencement of the long southbound climb over the Mendips. Note, on the extreme right, the WR Frome to Bristol branch line, from which passenger services had been withdrawn the previous November. *14th May 1960*

Four months later, the Stephenson Locomotive Society organised a special which included a run southwards over the S&D from Bath as far as Templecombe. For this trip, No. 53804, one of the original members of the class, was used. This special was run on a Sunday when there happened to be an engineering occupation of the Down line between Chilcompton and Binegar. On reaching Chilcompton, the train had to set back onto the Up line and proceed 'wrong road' for 2½ miles to Binegar, where it is seen re-crossing to the Down line. The pilotman, with his red armband, who accompanied the wrong line working, is about to climb down from the footplate. Standing in the Down line, a member of staff waits to unclip the points following the passage of the train. The unique S&D Class '7F' 2-8-0s were usually the 'number one' choice of motive power requested for tours over the line during the early 1960s. *11th September 1960*

WHIT SUNDAY EXCURSION

Since passing Radstock, now more than 4½ miles distant, BR Class '4' 4-6-0 No. 75072 and Class '5' 4-6-0 No. 73019 had already lifted their heavy train more than 400 feet to reach this location on the approach to Moorewood Sidings, between Chilcompton and Binegar. The rear of the train, a Whit Sunday excursion from Cheltenham to Bournemouth, can be seen emerging from the Down line portal of bridge No. 57, Burnt House Bridge, at Old Down. Despite overcoming the worst of the southbound ascent, there was still around another 2½ miles of climbing to reach the summit of the line near Masbury, much of it at 1 in 63/67. Norman obtained this view having reached the lineside from the next overbridge, Coal Lane Bridge (No. 58). *5th June 1960*

Norman recorded the lighting here as '*very dim*' and perhaps that is why he never printed this image. However, we just had to include it, as one of those occasions when his great friend Ivo Peters was 'captured' by the lineside. Standing beside milepost 22, Ivo gives a wave to the crew of BR Class '9F' 2-10-0 No. 92204 with the 8.40am (S.O.) Bournemouth- Bradford. The location is the long cutting near Cannards Grave, just to the south of Shepton Mallet. Here, after just a few dozen more yards, northbound trains completed the first part of the long climb from Evercreech Junction. There then followed a brief respite through Shepton Mallet, before climbing recommenced in earnest for the final 3¼ miles up to Masbury summit. *25th June 1960*

A BUSY DAY FOR NO. 92204

Later the same day and with the lighting only a little improved, No. 92204 returns southwards with the 7.45am (SO) Bradford-Bournemouth. Having just called at Templecombe Upper station and been drawn back down to the S&D main line at Templecombe No. 2 Junction, the train gathers speed down the gradient past the motive power depot and heads for the first crossing loop at Stalbridge. Notice, Ivo is again 'in shot', standing adjacent to the signal post on the spur leading up from No. 2 Junction to the Upper station on the Salisbury-Exeter main line. *25th June 1960*
The brick-built running shed seen here in the right background had only been erected at the start of the 1950s, provided to replace an earlier, much delapidated wooden structure. Norman doesn't appear to have been much attracted to visiting motive power depots; not, that is, until he started occasionally to photograph the S&D in 35mm colour. Perhaps it was the bulkiness of his large format press camera and boxes of glass plate negatives which deterred earlier visits.

AROUND TEMPLECOMBE NO. 2 JUNCTION

Without repeating too much detail which has been published before, the various Somerset & Dorset signal boxes at Templecombe were, by 1933, reduced to just one – Templecombe No. 2 Junction. Belatedly, the box was renamed Templecombe Junction. Even so, it appears that most people continued to refer to the box, and the junction at which it was located, by the former title – so that is the title I have used herein!

After the line closed in 1966, the removal of the Templecombe Junction nameplate from the front of the box revealed the original Templecombe No. 2 Junction board still in position underneath! I wonder if it still exists today?

Having just entered the single line section and commenced the descent southwards from No. 2 Junction, Class '2P' 4-4-0 No. 40563 has been retained ahead of modified 'West Country' No. 34039 *Boscastle* with the Down 'Pines Express'. Normal procedure was to remove the assisting locomotive at Evercreech Junction, so this unusual arrangement was possibly the result of the 'Bulleid' not performing too well. However, if this had been the case, Norman's photograph indicated that No. 34039 had more than regained her breath and she is seen here 'blowing off' from the safety valves. So, more likely, the '2P' had remained coupled to save a separate light engine movement to Bournemouth on a busy summer Saturday. The low angle of the photograph graphically illustrates the steepness of the line linking the original formation of the Dorset Central Railway with the spur put in later to provide a direct connection to the London & South Western Railway station on the Salisbury to Exeter main line. *25th June 1960*

The reporting number carried by the Class '2P' here means nothing to me. I wondered if Norman Lockett had misrecorded details of the train but a cross-check shows that Ivo Peters also had this in his notebook as being the 'Pines'. Perhaps the locomotive had carried this earlier in the day whilst heading a relief train?

No. 34039 is another of the Bulleid 'Light Pacifics' to be restored to working order after being saved from cutting up for scrap. Built at Brighton Works in 1946 and rebuilt (to the form seen above) at Eastleigh during 1959, the locomotive was transferred to Bournemouth, remaining there until a final reallocation, to Eastleigh in September 1962. Following withdrawal in May 1965, this 'Light Pacific' was taken to Woodham's scrapyard at Barry. Salvation came when No. 34039 became the first main line steam locomotive to arrive at Loughborough in January 1973 after the formation of the preservation society for the Great Central Railway. Following full restoration, Boscastle was returned to traffic in 1992. Still at the GCR, having been available for use during most of the remainder of the 1990s, No. 34039 is currently awaiting major repair works.

With so many Bulleids saved for restoration, I may not be alone in wishing that just one of the fine old ex-LM&S Class '2P' 4-4-0s had been saved; what a wonderful sight that would have made today – especially if painted in S&DJR Prussian Blue livery and numbered 45! A few years ago, a proposal was mooted to build a completely new locomotive of this class but, sadly, insufficient interest was shown. Still, with a number of such 'new build' schemes now in being, who knows, maybe one day …

Thirty minutes after the passage of the Bradford-Bournemouth train behind No. 92204 (page 137), BR Class '4' 4-6-0 No. 75073 appeared from Stalbridge with the 3.40pm Bournemouth-Bristol. This service was also booked to call at the Upper station, so will come to a halt at Templecombe No. 2 Junction, prior to being drawn in reverse up the spur line, seen to the right, by the station pilot. The rails to the left served the motive power depot and the former Lower Yard and this view gives another good indication of the different levels of the various lines. Notice the pouch containing the Stalbridge-Templecombe single line tablet extended from the side of the cab of No. 75073, ready to be 'caught' by the lineside catcher at No. 2 Junction. *25th June 1960*

We move back in time a few years here, to show a lineside view of the same location as appears overleaf. On an overcast Saturday afternoon, BR Class '5' 4-6-0 No. 73052 heads an eight-coach train between Cheriton Crossing and the former Templecombe No. 3 Junction. Norman had this noted as the 10.10am Sheffield Midland-Bournemouth – but this was shown in the WTT as the timing for the MFO working, the train booked to run around thirty minutes earlier on Saturdays. If I am correct, the train was here running about 8 mins down on schedule. *29th September 1956*

No doubt with an eye on the rapidly changing lighting as a storm brewed from the west, Norman was leaning against the northern parapet of Horsington Bridge (No. 146) to obtain this view. This is another example of where the two tracks diverge slightly, to enable each line to pass through its own portal at this two-arched structure. Unusually, the southbound 'Pines' is again double-headed south of Evercreech Junction. Class '2P' 4-4-0 No. 40569 and a BR Class '5' 4-6-0, both with a surplus of steam, reduce speed on the approach towards Templecombe No. 2 Junction and the start of the single line section towards Blandford. Notice the 'Limit of Shunt' indicator between the tracks, which applied to shunting movements from the Lower Yard, entry to which (at the former Templecombe No. 3 Junction) was gained just a little to the south of the overbridge from which Norman obtained this photograph. *1st August 1960*

WINCANTON DEPARTURE

The 3.40pm Bournemouth-Bristol features again, this time in the charge of No. 75072, another of Bath's allocation of the BR Class '4' 4-6-0s, here getting back into full stride having just called at Wincanton station. This attractive location is Plumer's Bridge (No. 131), just over half a mile further north, with the arm and upper post of Wincanton Down distant signal visible beyond. *1st August 1960*

Many pictures have appeared in print of northbound trains as seen approaching the southern face of this overbridge; in fact, in this shot, Ivo Peters can be seen doing just that! However, this is the only photograph I can recall having seen which was taken from this viewpoint. Unfortunately, it does not appear that Norman ever made a return visit here. It may be noticed that much of Bath's allocation of motive power was, by this time, beginning to suffer from a distinct lack of external cleanliness. This was, I suspect, a reflection on the difficulties of attracting school leavers into the motive power department by the early 1960s, an era when – believe it or not – most youngsters might prefer the advantages offered by an office or modern factory environment and at a time when such jobs were plentiful.

SUMMER 1961
THE END OF A LONG TRADITION

It was circumstantial that the first and last examples of the Class '2P' 4-4-0s to be built by the LM&S came to be allocated to the S&D – No. 563 (built 1928) from December 1947 and No. 700 (built 1932) from June 1936. Both were in service on the line until 1962. Here, No. 40563 gets back into her stride after calling at Binegar with the 3.20pm Bath-Templecombe and is about to pass under Gollidge's Bridge (No. 66), some half a mile short of Masbury summit. Coincidently, this appears to have been the member of the class photographed most often by Norman Lockett. This, however, proved to be the final time he captured her, before withdrawal from service from Templecombe some fourteen months later. *4th March 1961*

Locomotives of the 4-4-0 wheel arrangement first graced the metals of the S&D in 1891, when the first four examples delivered to the line began to take over the fast and semi fast duties which, until that time, had been the province of 0-6-0s and subsequently, 0-4-4Ts. The 4-4-0s, in their various forms, continued with the heaviest of the passenger trains, sometimes, as we have seen earlier in these pages, working in pairs or paired with an 0-6-0, until after the arrival of the Stanier Class '5' 4-6-0s. Thereafter, the main duties of the Class '2P's were to work the local and some of the semi-fast services, and to act as assisting locomotives to the 'Pines' and many of the summer Saturday through trains.

In 1951, there were still twelve of these locomotives at work on the S&D (No's 40505/9/63/4/8/9, with 40601/34/96/7/8 and 700), all of which we have featured in this book. Despite a few reallocations to replace withdrawals from service during the 1950s, by the start of 1961 the total had reduced to seven. This was the consequence of many of their duties having been taken over by the

BR Class '4' 4-6-0s, together with a diminishing need for double-heading. Thus 1961 proved to be the final summer when these grand old locomotives – so very much a part of the S&D – would provide assisting services. A further engine was withdrawn in October 1961 but, rather surprisingly, an ex-MR example, No. 40537, which had left Templecombe the previous year, was allocated back as late as February 1962. This locomotive lasted only a few months because, by September 1962, all had gone; the last, No. 40700, having been the final example of the class to be constructed by the LM&SR in 1932. To my mind, the loss of these 4-4-0s confirmed the beginning of the end for, without their deep and very steady 'woof' (never a bark!) echoing across the Somerset countryside, the S&D was never quite the same again. Their steadfast exhaust, seemingly never to miss a beat, especially when piloting a light-footed Bulleid 'Pacific' away from Evercreech Junction, was proof of their great value to the S&D. Thank goodness, some of their efforts were recorded on tape by Peter Handford in the 1950s and can still be heard today on CD.

The southbound 'Pines Express', complete with a full set of carriage boards, commences the climb away from Midford. It is a hot, cloudless, summer afternoon, hence there is barely any indication of exhaust from either Class '2P' No. 40634 or 'West Country' 4-6-2 No. 34043 *Combe Martin*. The 4-4-0, by this date the sole survivor of the trio of this class as supplied new to the S&DJR in 1928, was still allocated regularly in 1960 to the role of 'Pines Assist'. The locomotive was finally withdrawn from service from Templecombe shed in February 1962. The 'West Country', built in 1946, lasted only 2¼ years beyond No. 40634. Her claim to fame was to be the first of the class to have the original style of high-sided tender cut down in the spring of 1952. As such, she was instantly recognisable as the locomotive which was featured, just a few weeks later, crossing Midford Viaduct in the opening scene of that classic film *The Titfield Thunderbolt*! *24th June 1961*

No. 34043 may have been the 'No. 1 choice' for allocation to S&D duties by Bournemouth Central shed in 1961 because, as we shall see on some of the following pages, the locomotives features regularly – perhaps too regularly! Or was it that Norman Lockett's visits just happened to coincide with yet another trip over the Mendips by this member of the 'West Country' Class? Branksome footplateman Peter Smith, when working as fireman to driver Donald Beale, described No. 34043 as 'a strong engine for her class but rather a poor steamer'. In the first of his two books, Mendips Engineman *and* Footplate Across The Mendips*, Peter graphically describes a journey with No. 34043, working unassisted with the 2.52pm ex-Bath (the relief to the Down 'Pines') with a load of nine coaches – one over the limit for a class of locomotive renowned for light-footedness', a trait not partiuclarly conducive to the Bath-Evercreech Junction section of the S&D.

Returning to Norman Lockett's photograph, notice how the removal of the lineside hut which had housed Midford 'B' Ground Frame, provided the opportunity of an uninterrupted view across the viaduct when wishing to capture to film (or glass plate!) a southbound train from this level. Previously, photographers were faced with a choice of positioning themselves 'further up the lane' (to obtain the view more traditionally associated with this location) or – providing one held the appropriate photographic permit – immediately to the side of the Up line. Another option, featured within this book, was to walk a little further down the hill and photograph the train before it drew level to the position of the ground frame. All of which reminds me, although not necessarily appropriate at this location, there was a method, which Ivo Peters sometimes encouraged Norman to use when, together, the two friends visited the lineside. There were a number of locations from which a better view could be had by means of a little 'additional elevation' – and that was obtained by standing on the boot of Ivo's Bentley! The view looking north adjacent to the lineside near the entrance to Midford Goods Yard was one such example when the vegetation had grown a little too high to enable a clear shot to be had from 'terra firma'.

Elsewhere in this book, I make reference to the railway cottage occupied by Midford signalman Percy Savage and its close proximity to the box where he worked for so many years, until the closure of the line in March 1966. Well, there is the cottage, seen to the left of the viaduct in this view. It's still there today, the only reminder of its earlier S&D associations being the wooden bargeboards on one of the gable ends – the pattern matches exactly that which had adorned some of the Somerset & Dorset Railway's signal boxes!

* Such was the popularity of Peter's two books, they were subsequently reissued in 1987 by the Oxford Publishing Company as a combined edition, bearing the title The Somerset & Dorset From The Footplate.

The view northwards from Templecombe No. 2 Junction Signal Box, with the signal giving the road directly onto the single line all but obscured by the exhaust of BR Class '5' 4-6-0 No. 73050. This train, which had slowed to observe the 20mph speed restriction, was the 9.30am (summer Sundays) Bristol to Bournemouth. This service omitted the time-consuming call at Templecombe Upper station and was booked to run non-stop from Wincanton to Sturminster Newton. 20th August 1961

Note the level of what had been the original S&D main line to the right of this view, now serving as the access to the motive power depot and the former Lower Yard. From 1870, trains climbed from the lower level, at what became Templecombe No. 3 Junction, to reach the L&SWR main line station. Part way along the new spur, No. 2 Junction was created, permitting trains to be diverted onto the start of a single line. This, in turn, descended back to the lower level and rejoined the original formation, at No. 1 Junction, before the S&DJR passed, at right angles, under the Salisbury-Exeter main line. No. 1 Junction lasted only until 1877, whereas the control of No. 3 Junction was incorporated into the signal box at No. 2 Junction by the Southern Railway in 1933. No. 73050 was purchased privately following withdrawal and donated to Peterborough City Council, who leased the locomotive to the Nene Valley Railway where it remains based to date. First steamed in preservation in 1972, the locomotive is currently out of traffic undergoing major repairs.

BR Class '4' 4-6-0 No. 75027 and rebuilt SR 'Light Pacific' No. 34028 *Eddystone* **slow on the approach to Shepton Mallet (Charlton Road) station. Here, the 10.38am (SO) Manchester-Bournemouth made a scheduled stop. Prominent in the left foreground is the tall Up starting signal. The elevated arm was necessary to provide a good sighting for the footplate crews of Up through trains before passing under the station footbridge, from where Norman obtained this photograph. Shepton Mallet was one of the few more important places through which the S&D passed. Even so, much of its rail business was the province of the former GWR, whose station was more conveniently situated for the town. However, neither station survived the Beeching axe.** *2nd September 1961*
Both of these locomotives survived into preservation, No. 75027 at the Bluebell Railway, whilst No. 34028 is owned by Southern Locomotives Ltd and currently based at the Swanage Railway. In November 2006, forty-five years after Norman took this photograph, they could again be seen working together during an S&D Special Weekend on the Bluebell line.

RIGHT: For the 1961 and '62 summer seasons, Bath shed again received an allocation of four of the BR Class '9F' 2-10-0s; No's 92000/1/6/12 in 1961 and 92201/10/33/45 the following year. No. 92001 is here about to enter the 440 yards long Devonshire Tunnel with the 7.43am (SO) Bradford-Bournemouth service. *14th July 1962*

The overbridge in the background is Maple Grove Bridge (No. 9), which carried a public footpath over the line and was a favourite location from which to watch or photograph trains climbing Devonshire bank. It survives to this day, now crossing the linear footpath laid out on much of the former route of the S&D between Bath Junction and Devonshire Tunnel. The cutting here was partially infilled, sufficiently high to cover the blocked up mouth of Devonshire Tunnel. However, as revealed in the caption to the final photograph in this book, this is about to be reversed, with the proposed reopening of both Devonshire and Combe Down tunnels.

ROCK CUTTING BRIDGE

Many of the overbridges and tunnels on the S&D had a restricted headroom; Devonshire and Combe Down tunnels, for example, provided less than twelve inches clearance above the top of the chimney of some classes of locomotive! However, one overbridge, quite untypical by S&D standards, was 'Rock Cutting Bridge' (No. 127,) which carried a public road across the line near Shepton Montague, between Cole and Wincanton. Sometimes unofficially referred to as 'the high-arched bridge', the two portals were recorded as having a height of 21 feet 2 inches from rail level to the soffits of the arches.

'Armstrong' Class '4F' 0-6-0 No. 44559 passes under Bridge No. 127 with a Down local service and completes a half mile climb graded at 1 in 100; the gradient post, seen end on in the left foreground, marking the point where the formation changed to 1 in 116 falling towards Wincanton. In comparison with the severity of the hill climbing north of Evercreech Junction, the gradients on this part of the line were nowhere near so severe, two short sections of 1 in 80 being the maximum between 'the Junction' and Templecombe. However the profile of the line was ever changing. *7th July 1962*
The second arch of Bridge 127 was added when this section of the line was doubled by the S&DJR in 1884, the original Dorset Central line having been single since services commenced in 1862. Look carefully and you can see the 'join', made more pronounced because, whilst the Down line arch crossed the railway on the skew, the Up side structure sat square across the line. This was no doubt done to minimise any change to the direction of the roadway above, when the second set of rails were added.

BELOW: Abstract from the *BR (Western Region) Sectional Appendix (Bristol Traffic District – October 1960)* **listing inclines steeper than 1 in 200. The top two entries refer to the gradients mentioned in the above photograph.**

Incline between		Distance about	Gradient 1 in	Falling towards	
Cole and Wincanton	..	60 ch.	100	Cole	.. ..
Cole and Wincanton	..	40 ch.	116	Wincanton.	
Cole and Wincanton	..	1 mile	133	Cole	.. ..
Cole and Wincanton	..	40 ch.	152	Cole	.. ..
Cole and Wincanton	..	30 ch.	100	Wincanton	.. ..

Looking now towards the northern face of the bridge, BR Class '3' 2-6-2T No. 82001 heads towards Cole with a Templecombe-Highbridge service. The Western Region introduced a few examples of this class to the S&D after taking over responsibility for the motive power for the line, No. 82001 having been transferred to Templecombe in March/April 1961. After just two years, the locomotive was transferred away to Exmouth Junction, no doubt to see action on the East Devon branch line services. After further moves to Taunton and Bristol, Barrow Road, I think No. 82001 did find her way to Bath Green Park shed late in 1965, only to be withdrawn from service in December that same year. *7th July 1962*

EVERCREECH JUNCTION

The Collett '22xx/32xx' 0-6-0s were another former GW class, examples of which were brought to the line following transfer of responsibility of S&D motive power to the Western Region. Principally, they were seen as a replacement for the former LM&S/S&D Class '3F' 0-6-0s still at work but which, by the start of the 1960s, had reached the stage where withdrawal from service of these elderly engines was becoming inevitable. The first of the Collett 0-6-0s to be allocated to the S&D was No. 3218, sent to Templecombe in April 1960 (coincidentally as a direct replacement for Class '3F' No. 43218). Over the following five and a quarter years, at one time or another, around twenty of these locomotives saw service over the S&D. Norman Lockett was lucky to capture No. 2277 at work, as this proved to be one of the shortest allocations to the line, the engine arriving at Templecombe in November 1961 and transferring away again during November 1962. Here, the 0-6-0 waits at Evercreech Junction with the 2.20pm Highbridge-Templecombe, the 22¼ mile journey completed thus far having taken one minute short of the hour. Departure from 'the Junction' was scheduled for 3.23pm and, after calling at Cole and Wincanton, Tmeplecombe was reached some twenty-four minutes later, thus equating to an overall average speed of around 23mph; just about right if you were not in any sort of hurry and wanted to enjoy the ever changing views from the window of a compartment which, more than likely, you might have all to yourself! *1st September 1962*
Note the doorway to the two-storey, stationmaster's house, surrounded by climbing roses. The staff at Evercreech Junction, like those at many of the S&D stations, put considerable effort into ensuring a proliferation of colour each summer, with impressive flower beds, hanging baskets and even a bowl of flowers in the waiting room. The staff here vied with colleagues up and down the line (especially at Midsomer Norton) for the much coveted certificate of 'Best Kept Station' and those who have watched the programme of (the late) Sir John Betjeman's visit here might recall seeing just such a certificate, framed and proudly displayed on the waiting room wall.

The movement of locomotives to and from the Middle Siding at Evercreech Junction (which lay between the Up and Down running lines – see page 131, top picture), resulted in the introduction of a number of local 'whistle codes', to indicate to the signalman of the South Box the required movement of a light engine. These codes, the first of which should correctly read as 'Up Line to Middle Road', were still quoted in the 1960 *Sectional Appendix to the Bristol Traffic District Working Time Tables* as below:
I am not sure how often they were actually used; presumably only should the signalman have set the various points for something other than where the driver was expecting to go! Of my own all too rare visits here on a summer Saturday, I have no recollections of a plethora of whistling. In any case, just a few days after Norman took the above picture, the requirement for these codes would become all but superfluous, with the withdrawal of the 'Pines' and the summer through traffic and, with them, the loss of the assisting locomotive duties over the Mendip Hills to and from Bath.

Evercreech Jn. South ..	Up line Middle road.	1 short, 2 short.
	Middle road to yard.	1 short, 1 long.
	Down line to Middle road.	1 short, 3 short.
	From Middle road when ready to set back to up train.	4 long.
	From middle road when ready to set back to Down train.	5 long.

The afternoon calm of a sunny Sunday at 'the Junction' is disturbed by Class '4F' 0-6-0 No. 44560 in charge of an engineering train. As I remarked earlier, with most of the S&D closed to all traffic on Sundays following cessation of the Summer WTT, this was always the ideal opportunity to undertake engineering works. If the task involved some major relaying project, it was not unknown to assemble some 60 men or more who would be transported to the site, the work perhaps extending over a number of consecutive Sundays. This also meant calling out signalmen for the key boxes, often to open for the outward passage of the engineer's train then, later in the day, to repeat the exercise to accommodate the return working. It was sometimes a matter of debate as to whether this opportunity for a signalman to add very little to the basic weekly wage was judged as sufficient recompense for the inconvenience incurred on what might otherwise have been a 'rest day'! *30th September 1962*

S&D Class '7F' 2-8-0s Still Hard at Work

ABOVE: By the summer of 1962, the regular (but not quite exclusive) motive power acting as assisting locomotives to the 'Pines' and the Saturday through trains, were the BR Standard Class '4' 2-6-0s and 4-6-0s. Norman Lockett did not record the identities of the two locomotives seen here on the climb from Bath Junction towards Devonshire Tunnel but it has been reported elsewhere that they were No. 75009 coupled ahead of S&D Class '7F' No. 53806. Earlier in the summer, this service, the 7.00am Cleethorpes to Exmouth and Sidmouth, had been the province of a Class '4F' 0-6-0 with assistance from a BR Class '4' but on at least two Saturdays during August 1962, a '7F' 2-8-0 was allocated to the train. The 'pilot' was returning to Templecombe, having assisted the northbound 'Pines Express' from Evercreech Junction to Bath earlier in the day. *25th August 1962*
The three photographs featured on these two pages are from the autumn of 1962, by which date all six of the original 1914 series of the S&D Class '7F' 2-8-0s had been withdrawn but all five of the 1925-built locomotives remained in service. The hard work to which they continued to be put only served to hasten their eventual withdrawal; the first to go, No. 53810, succumbed at the end of 1963, the remainder following by the end of October 1964. So how fortuitous that, out of a class which totalled only eleven, two were destined to be saved and restored, and continue to be seen at work on heritage lines into the 21st century. As an aside, whilst not into railway modelling myself, I am amazed that, bearing in mind the level of interest, none of the commercial manufacturers has yet produced a 'ready to run' 00 gauge model to satisfy the many people who would clamour for both the original and later, larger diameter variants of these wonderful old stalwarts. Come to think of it, I suspect the appeal to own just such a model might extend beyond the modelling fraternity; after all these were very special locomotives on a very special line!

OPPOSITE PAGE BOTTOM: The Up service of the 'Cleethorpes' over the S&D was more was regularly rostered for a '7F' and here No. 53810 heads eastwards from Wellow. Earlier in this book, I mentioned the overall timing of these services was about ten hours! From memory, this never improved but did anybody, other, perhaps, than a dedicated railway enthusiast, really ever travel all the way from Cleethorpes to spend a holiday in Bournemouth (or, come to that, even in the opposite direction!)? *1st September 1962*
Notice how little has changed since Norman's first visit to this same location in 1936 (see page 15); on the face of it, only some twenty-six years of tree growth, which now obscures more of the view from here of the tower of St Julian's Church.

RIGHT: Another Sunday Rail Tour, this one organised by the Locomotive Club of Great Britain, led to the inevitable request for an S&D '7F' to be provided for at least a part of the itinerary. No. 53808 duly supplied the motive power for the journey from Broadstone to Bath, with a break at Evercreech Junction whilst the special made a return run along the branch to Highbridge behind ex-GW 0-6-0 No. 3210. Having just taken over the special again, No. 53808 sets off for the return run to Bath. *30th September 1962*

The most optimistic diehards were, by September 1962, beginning to accept the inevitability that the S&D was doomed for closure within just a few more years. However, who, in their wildest dreams, could have imagined that, nearly fifty years later, old No. 88 (No. 53808's original guise) would be busy at work hauling trainloads of passengers to the seaside in Somerset! So how much longer before No. 88 revisits old haunts, even if initially it might just be a weekend spent steaming for less than a mile 'up the bank' from Midsomer Norton station?

Autumn was in the air as No. 53809 plodded over Portway Bridge (No. 62) and climbed towards Binegar (a little more than a half mile further south) with the 8.55am Bath-Evercreech Junction freight. This heavy train required the assistance of a banker. One of Radstock's small allocation of Class '3F' 0-6-0s can be seen at the rear and, judging from the exhaust, was going flat out in full forward gear! By this point in the southbound climb, the worst of the gradients had been left behind. However, there were still another 1¾ miles to the summit near Masbury, most of it exposed to the strong cross-winds which often blow across the Mendip Hills from the Bristol Channel. *6th October 1962*

MODIFIED BULLEIDS

The exhaust from hard-working rebuilt 'West Country' No. 34039 *Boscastle* is deposited liberally across the Up side of the line as one of Templecombe's BR Class '4' 4-6-0s, No. 75009, assists the Bulleid 'Light Pacific' on the long hard slog up towards Chilcompton Tunnel. The train is the Down 'Pines Express' and judging from Norman's recorded time for this picture, it was running hard to make up for a late arrival into Bath from the north. *23rd June 1962*

During this last summer of S&D through Saturday holiday traffic, the Bulleid 'Light Pacifics' from Bournemouth shed were still a regular sight over the Mendips. Here, rebuilt 'West Country' No. 34040 *Crewkerne*, piloted by one of Bath's BR Class '5' 4-6-0s, No. 73054, emerge from Devonshire Tunnel with the 12.20pm (SO) Bournemouth -Nottingham. Notice, by the way, just how tight was the fit of a train with the bore of this notorious tunnel. *14th July 1962*

Unmodified 'Light Pacific' No. 34043 *Combe Martin* has the assistance of another of Bath's BR Class '5's, No. 73049, on the long northbound climb from Evercreech Junction. Here, three miles into the climb, the pair pass over the elegant eleven arch Prestleigh Viaduct with the 12.20pm (SO) Bournemouth-Nottingham. This viaduct, about mid-way between Evercreech New and Shepton Mallet, was situated on a stretch of unbroken gradient of 1 in 50, which extended from Evercreech New up to Cannards Grave. *7th July 1962*

Harking back to my comment a few pages earlier, here is No. 34043 *Combe Martin* again, this time in company with BR Class '4' 4-6-0 No. 75027 and in charge of the 10.55am (SO) Manchester-Bournemouth. The view is from the cutting at Old Down, immediately to the north of Burnt House Bridge (No. 57), the passage of which heralded the end of the 1 in 50 sections of the southbound climb. The Chilcompton Up distant signal is visible as the line curves from view in the background. *14th July 1962*

1962 – VARIETY STILL THE WATCHWORD

Ironically, it was as late as 1961 in the history of the S&D that the lineside observer was to witness the greatest variety of motive power ever to be seen working over the route. Even the following summer, the last for through holiday traffic, provided a good selection of locomotives, although by this date, BR Standard types were of the majority, whilst the former GWR '22xx' Class now worked many of the local trains both on the branch and, to a lesser extent, on the main line.

However, as mentioned earlier, by September 1962 the very last of the Class '2P' 4-4-0s had been retired, to which must also be

added the final example, on the S&D, of a Class '3F' 0-6-0 'Bulldog' and two of the former S&D Class '4F' 0-6-0 'Armstrongs'. Thus the character of the motive power on the S&D, so long associated with the designs of the former Midland and LM&S railways, was continuing to change, now ever more rapidly. However, as we shall see later, amongst the types still yet to appear, one class at least was of Stanier design. On a brighter note, albeit temporarily, for the third successive summer, four BR 'Nines' were allocated to Bath: No's 92201/10/33/45 of which No. 92210 was replaced, in August, by No. 92220 *Evening Star*.

If you have watched the wonderful cine films of the S&D taken by Ivo Peters, you may recognise this scene and recall how, as Ivo pans his camera around, a 'body' appears briefly but prominently in the foreground. That happened to be Norman Lockett, in the process of taking this very photograph! Here, the fourth of the 1962 quartet of BR Class '9F' 2-10-0s, emerges from Chilcompton Tunnel with the 7.45am (SO) Bradford-Bournemouth. The happy and obliging crew, in response to a pre-arranged request, were determined to be captured on celluloid and, in Norman's case, on glass plate. *23rd June 1962*
Notice, by the way, the temporary speed restriction sign on the Up road. For as long as I can recall on the S&D, there were many periods when the section of line between Chilcompton Tunnel and Radstock appeared to suffer such restrictions, often the consequence of some slippage and the repairs which followed. More recently, as the S&DJR Heritage Trust strive to advance their rails further southwards from Midsomer Norton station, it is evident that such slippage has continued to effect the line of the old formation over the many intervening years.

The signalman at Midsomer Norton South watches from his box as BR Class '4' 4-6-0 No. 75023 and an unidentified BR Class '5' pound their way through the station with the southbound 'Pines Express'. *19th May 1962*
I cannot let pass the opportunity to comment on the box at Midsomer Norton South. The structure seen here was demolished following closure of the S&D but, in 2007, a superb near-replica replacement structure was completed by a very small nucleus of members (basically two!) of the S&DR Heritage Trust, which has its headquarters at this station. I hope this picture (deliberately selected as a double page spread for them) will serve as a tribute to their Herculean efforts. Whilst not yet operationally complete, hopefully, in the near future, the box will control the movements of a fledgling rail passenger service, albeit initially running less than a mile towards Chilcompton. However, it is the beginnings of an exciting project, which most people (myself included) would have imagined impossible not many years previously. Indeed, since I first drafted this caption, I have experienced 'pulling off' the first of the reinstalled and reconnected signals, the Up starter, an earlier version of which can be seen in the middle background of Norman's photograph!

NEAR SHEPTON MONTAGUE

This was yet another very picturesque section of the line, running south-eastwards from Wyke Champflower, through Cole and passing the hamlets of Pitcombe and Shepton Montague, before the rails skirted the racecourse, high above the line, on the approach to Wincanton.

Just to the east of Shepton Montague, the line entered a short but substantial rock cutting which, judging from the width between the exposed sides, must have provided the builders of the Dorset Central Railway with a valuable source of stone for construction of some of the works. This section of the line was opened (as a single line) to public traffic on 3rd February 1862, by which date plans for amalgamation with the Somerset Central Railway were already well advanced; the Somerset & Dorset Railway came into being just

seven months later, on 1st September 1862. Unlike the Somerset Central, built as a broad gauge line as the consequence of its support by the Bristol & Exeter Railway, and later narrowed, this section of the line – being a part of the Dorset Central – was always narrow (*i.e.* standard) gauge.

By the way, the high overbridge in the background of the view opposite features in more detail on pages 146-147 and, I suspect, the original single arched structure may well have been built using this local source of stone. Little more than a mile to the east of this point stands Redlynch House and parklands, and although it is said these features could be glimpsed from a passing train, the author doubts this claim on the basis he himself never once caught sight of the mansion!

BR Class '4' 4-6-0 No. 75027 and the now familiar No. 34043 *Combe Martin* **run at speed south of Pitcombe towards the rock cutting near Shepton Montague. The train is the 10.30am (SO) Manchester-Bournemouth and both locomotives appear to be consuming coal of dubious quality! Notice how the exhaust of the BR Standard is thrown vertically whilst that from the 'Bulleid' hangs much closer to the locomotive.** *7th July 1962*

The long embankment, seen here, preceded the southbound approach to the rock cutting featured on the following three pages. The camera angle has the effect of foreshortening the underbridge partially obscured by the lineside tree. This was actually a three arch bridge, which was also the official title bestowed on the structure, No. 126 in the S&D Bridge List! Originally provided because the railway had bisected the local farmer's lands, one arch of the bridge also spanned a stream, which meandered northwards for a couple more miles before joining the River Brue, near Cole.

Norman moved a couple of hundred yards south for this next shot, as BR Class '5' No. 73051 curves through the rock cutting near Shepton Montague with the 3.40pm Bournemouth-Bristol, a service which, over the years, has been referred to as the 'Up Mail'. *7th July 1962*

Many years ago, whilst we were both involved with making two television programmes about the S&D, the well-known Branksome engineman Peter Smith pointed out to me that, whilst the 3.40pm did indeed convey mail, it was the evening freight from Poole, together with the 2.40am from Bath, which were invariably referred to by S&D staff as the 'Up' and 'Down Mails'! Ironically, however, the Up freight from Poole did not carry mail traffic, at least, not during the era of which I have memories of the S&D.

Turning around to look in the opposite direction from the previous photograph, ex-GWR Collett 0-6-0 No. 3216, allocated to the S&D in October 1960 until withdrawn towards the end of 1963, was captured making her leisurely way southwards with the 3.20pm Highbridge-Templecombe. *7th July 1962*

BR Class '9F' No. 92245 climbs Devonshire Bank with the 7.45am (SO) Bradford-Bournemouth. Bath Green Park station was located off beyond the right edge of this photograph and this will give some indication of just how far the single line has changed in direction in little more than a mile since diverging from the Midland route at Bath Junction. The long straight here carried the line up to the entrance of Devonshire Tunnel. *28th July 1962*

No. 92245 was purchased as one of the 'Barry Ten', being amongst the last locomotives to be removed from Woodham's Yard in 1988 and placed in the ownership of the Vale of Glamorgan Council. The locomotive awaits restoration and is stored at the ex-EWS depot at the Barry Island Railway.

AN EXCITING FINALÉ

In August 1962, No. 92210 was returned by Bath shed in exchange for No. 92220 *Evening Star*, the last steam locomotive to be constructed by BR at Swindon Works in March 1960, and turned out with a fully lined green livery and complete with a copper topped chimney. It was transferred to the S&D especially to work the final runs, via the S&D route, of the 'Pines Express'.

RIGHT: No. 92220 on the 'Boat Road' at Bath shed. Ivo Peters had brought along his cine camera and was pictured by Norman, perched rather precariously filming a close-up of the nameplate on the smoke deflector plate of *Evening Star*.

After an initial 'spruce-up' by the cleaners at Bath shed, No. 92220 was given some outings over the S&D. Here, she climbs the gradient on the approach to the platform end at Evercreech New station with the 3.40pm Bournemouth-Bristol. Disregard, by the way, the reporting number; this referred to the earlier southbound working, the 9.03am Bristol-Bournemouth. *18th August 1962*

In order to minimise conflicting traffic flows over the single line sections on summer Saturdays, it was a long established practice to group southbound S&D departures from Bath to the very early hours of the day, then again from early afternoon, whilst the morning was used primarily for northbound traffic. The 3.40pm departure from Bournemouth did not fit into this pattern and three crossings had to be scheduled at intermediate stations on the single line between Blandford and Templecombe. Because the 3.40pm carried mail traffic and had to connect with the northern 'Postal' at Mangotsfield, it was given precedence over the southbound trains, including the 'Pines', which was scheduled to wait nearly ten minutes in the loop at Stalbridge to allow the Up train to pass. All too soon, however, with no through summer traffic and no 'Pines Express', this would be a problem no more.

No. 92220, given the name Evening Star *in recognition of being the last steam locomotive to be built by BR, is today part of the National Collection. After many years both on main line steam trips and on loan to various heritage railways, the locomotive is currently out of traffic and following some years on display at the National Railway Museum, York, was transferred to the STEAM Museum of the Great Western Railway at Swindon in early September 2008.*

The final Saturday of through traffic – and the very last 'Pines Express' to traverse the S&D. At lunch time, Ivo Peters had returned to Bath after a morning photographing the northbound 'Pines'. Having now met up with Ivo, Norman took a colour photograph of the southbound 'Pines' at Midsomer Norton. They then raced the train to Portway Bridge, between Chilcompton and Binegar. Here, Ivo left a nephew to operate his cine camera whilst he positioned himself a little to the south of where Norman took this superb study of *Evening Star* forging up the gradient towards Binegar. It is a totally different view to that taken by Ivo but if you look at his picture, you will see Norman, having already obtained his shot, waving from the lineside. The field on the left was awash with Ivo's relatives and friends, watching, filming and photographing the progress of No. 92220, so Norman did very well to obtain this view free of other lineside observers! *8th September 1962*

Norman later took a final photograph of the train as it passed Cole, by which stage the front of Evening Star had been adorned with a wreath, placed on the locomotive's smokebox whilst halted at Evercreech Junction. However, as Norman's photograph replicates exactly that already published by Ivo, we have omitted it here.

SECTION 6
1963-1966
RUNDOWN AND CLOSURE

I cannot remember now who first said, "*It was not the fact they closed the S&D that was so sad, it was the manner by which they did it.*" However, it is a sentiment with which I and, I suspect, many others who knew the line, concur. 'They' were generally regarded as the Western Region management of British Railways. The removal of the 'Pines Express', together with all of the other through summer Saturday trains from the S&D in early September 1962, was tantamount to inviting Dr Beeching to weald his infamous axe. Beeching duly obliged; in March 1963 his report, *The Reshaping of British Railways*, confirmed the S&D system should be included in the long list of closures which would decimate the railways of this country. Predictably, today we still live with the effects of this folly, especially following the great resurgence of railway travel in more recent years! However, never forget that, in the last resort, it was government policy which sounded the death knell for this famous old cross-country railway and, whilst it was a Conservative

administration that set the proposals for closure into motion, it was a newly-elected (old style) Labour government who steadfastly refused to reverse the decision.

From 1st January 1963, all Southern Region territory west of Wilton (just to the west of Salisbury), Blandford, and Dorchester was transferred to the Western Region. One outcome, later that same year, was the transfer of Templecombe shed from the Bristol (82) Division into the Exeter (83) Sub-District of the Plymouth Division. Locomotives allocated to Templecombe lost their '82G' shed plates, to be replaced by '83G'. On the S&D main line, the Western Region's ownership now extended almost as far south as Blandford Forum.

On a more personal note, I can still recall vividly my visits to Midford Signal Box in 1963 and how different was the atmosphere to just a few years earlier. Gone were the periods of organised (and, occasionally, disorganised) frenzy, to be replaced by long periods of inactivity punctuated by the passage of the occasional train. Now,

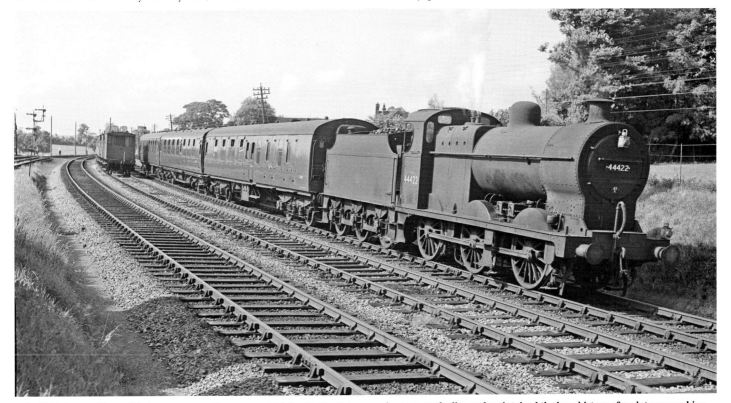

In 1964, it was still possible to see some motive power which harked back to a previous era on the line and maintained the long history of such types working in deepest Somerset and Dorset. Typical were the Class '4F' 0-6-0s, including this 'old faithful', No. 44422, here displaying an '83G' Templecombe shed code and slowing for the stop at Evercreech Junction with the 3.20pm Bath-Templecombe. Note the row of brake vans at the north end of the middle siding. The buffer stop to this siding included a coupling hook which could be used to secure any parked unfitted wagons from running away down the grade. More usually, the siding would also accommodate the Highbridge branch train between duties. *25th July 1964*

No. 4422 first transferred from Bristol Barrow Road to Bath in early March 1946 and remained throughout the 1950s, with periods on loan to Templecombe during 1959. In December 1959, an 'on-loan' transfer to Barrow Road resulted in the locomotive returning to Templecombe from late January/early February 1960. In November 1960, a visit was made to Derby Works for repairs, following which No. 44422 was officially allocated to Templecombe. It was from there, just a matter of weeks after Norman took this photograph, that the final departure from S&D metals was made, with a transfer first to Barrow Road, then, at the end of January 1965, to Gloucester. There, the locomotive was withdrawn from service during the week ending 22nd May 1965. Sold to Woodhams at Barry, No. 44422 made what was thought would be its final journey, from Gloucester, on 10th August 1965. However, it was destined to escape the cutter's torch. Restored to full working order at the Cheddleton Railway Centre of the (then) North Staffordshire Railway Society, in more recent times No. 44422 has paid visits to several other lines, including the West Somerset Railway.

the only regular traffic which appeared to galvanise the signalmen's special attention was the 'Perisher', the nightly service of perishables traffic which ran between Templecombe and Derby. However, at least in 1963 there was still some sort of nightly service, including the 'Down Mail', a rather grand title for a freight service which included a mails van! Even this, however, was soon to be withdrawn, as more and more of the freight traffic was run down or diverted to other routes. For example, the evening Poole-Bath freight, which had long included clay traffic from Dorset to the Staffordshire potteries, was withdrawn, the traffic reported as being diverted to run from Poole westwards along the south coast to Dorchester, where it was added to a Weymouth-Bristol service. It was seemingly a case of doing anything to ensure no regular through freight remained on the S&D line. So, from September 1964, the S&D closed at night. With the remnants of some local freight, which would soon be discontinued, only the movement of coal remained as a regular traffic. As coal production reduced in the remaining collieries served by the S&D in the North Somerset coalfield, even some of this once important traffic became more irregular.

The main interest, as far as the enthusiast was concerned, was the number of rail tours and specials which, first in anticipation and then later as a consequence of the confirmation of closure, visited the S&D. I have to admit that, during the last twelve months of the line's existence, I decided to stay away rather than to watch the final 'death throes'. All these years later, I remain undecided as to whether I made the right decision! However, in July 1964, I was at least able to organise a honeymoon in Bournemouth, which was reached, of course, via the S&D! It was just about my last happy memory of the line.

As with the preceding period in the history of the S&D, during those last few years – from 1963 to early 1966 – Norman Lockett frequently accompanied Ivo Peters to the lineside and the latter's published pictures have already featured much of what Norman also photographed. Likewise, many photographs have been published of others who recorded these last few years; indeed far more people than had ever shown much interest just a few years earlier, for – contrary to the impression sometimes now given – the fields adjoining the S&D were rarely 'awash with enthusiasts'; not that is, until the fate of the line had been announced. So, again, for this final period, when a loyal but disillusioned S&D staff still strove, against the odds, to provide a service to the public, we have attempted to limit Norman's pictures to a small selection which does not replicate, any more than is unavoidable, scenes which may been published already by others.

As mentioned in the Introduction to this book, Norman thought better of attempting to carry his large press camera and associated equipment to the lineside during the period at the start of 1963, when the S&D was overwhelmed by snow. He did accompany Ivo Peters into the Mendip Hills in early January 1963 but, wisely, carried only his 35mm camera with which he took seventeen colour transparencies!

By 1963, all of the original (1914) members of the S&D Class '7F' 2-8-0s had been withdrawn, whilst all of the later (1925) batch remained in service and could be seen hard at work, albeit the volume of freight traffic was now diminishing. It is often overlooked, however, that these locomotives were also diagrammed to spend some of their working day moving freight traffic via the former Midland lines north of Bath; usually trip workings to and from Westerleigh Sidings, Bristol (St Philips Yard) and, via the Clifton Down Line, Avonmouth Old Yard. Here, on more familiar territory, No. 53807 climbs past the entrance to Norton Hill Colliery just prior to reaching Midsomer Norton South station with the 11.00am Bath-Evercreech Junction freight. *27th September 1963*

The loading of some of the freight traffic was still sufficient to require the assistance of a banker from Bath Junction to Combe Down Tunnel and from Radstock to the summit of the line at Masbury. Fowler Class '3F' 0-6-0 No. 47557 is seen dropping off the rear of the 11.00am Bath-Evercreech Junction freight at the summit, with fireman Eric Wilson giving a cheery wave. The special uncoupling iron (seen hanging from the handrail on the smokebox door of No. 47557) was used by the guard to lift the three-link coupling and release the locomotive from the rear of the train. For a fuller description of the 'banking' procedure, refer back to page 17. *24th September 1963*
The Class '3F' 0-6-0 tanks first appeared on the S&D at the very end of 1928, the first of a batch of seven of these locomotives built by W.G. Bagnall Ltd of Stafford. Often referred to (some would argue erroneously) as 'Jinties', on the S&D they were known as 'Bagnalls'. No. 47557 arrived on the line in March 1942 and remained allocated at Bath or Radstock until withdrawn less than five months after photographed here. Perhaps that explains why the shedplate had already been removed.

THE CHANGING FACE OF FREIGHT TRAFFIC

S&D Class '7F' No. 53810 drifts slowly down the gradient past Midsomer Norton station with a morning freight service from Evercreech Junction to Bath. In December of the same year, No. 53810 became the first of the 1925 series of this unique class to be withdrawn from service. On the left stands NCB 0-6-0 saddle tank *Lord Salisbury*, which had paused between shunting duties at Norton Hill Colliery. The position of the NCB locomotive was somewhat further out from the colliery entrance gate towards the main line than would normally have been seen. Let's just say this was a case of 'by special arrangement' for the two photographers involved! *27th September 1963*

As an aside, I last saw Lord Salisbury, built in 1906 at Bristol by Peckett & Sons, in the station yard of my home town, having been purchased for cutting by the local scrap merchant.

As the S&D Class '7F' were reduced in numbers by scrapping, replacement motive power came in the form of the ex-LM&S Class '8F' 2-8-0s. It has been reported that, previously, three of this class were allocated to Bath for a short time during 1941. On the climb from Midford towards Combe Down Tunnel, No. 48468 passed Midford goods yard (soon to be closed) with the 6.25am Evercreech Junction-Bath freight. With the general run-down of steam, many locomotive transfers came about as the consequence of 'passing on' surplus stock. No. 48468 came to Bath Green Park from Kidderminster at the start of 1962 and was taken out of traffic and condemned in May 1964. *25th September 1963*

Notice how the iron boundary fence to the right was positioned well back from the line. This dated from 1892, when the additional strip of line was purchased in anticipation of the abortive proposals to extend the double track northwards from Midford to the approach to Combe Down Tunnel. The original iron fence (also repositioned in 1892) had been one of many requirements of the owner of Midford Castle Estate when the S&D first sought powers to build the line.

BRANCH LINE PASSENGER TRAFFIC

OPPOSITE PAGE TOP: Few photographs of the Evercreech-Highbridge line during the latter years appear in this book. Invariably, most of Norman's later visits to the branch were in the company of Ivo Peters, so, more usually, he used his 35mm colour camera. This exception features ex-GWR 0-6-0 No. 3210, making a spirited departure from West Pennard with the 2.20pm from Highbridge to Templecombe. Ivo can be seen on the Up platform. *7th September 1963*

It always surprised (and rather pleased) me that, right to the closure of the S&D, at West Pennard the Western Region painters never despoiled – other than the signal box – the Southern livery applied to all the buildings. Having said that, before closure the station was destined to lose its passing loop, signal box and goods facilities (although the goods shed and main station building remain to this day) and, as such, presented a very sad sight to those few passengers who still made some use of the railway, it being a climb of nearly a mile and a half to the centre of the village this station had been built to serve.

MAIN LINE LOCAL TRAFFIC

ABOVE: Crossing Midford Viaduct and with a full head of steam, BR Class '4' 4-6-0 No. 75073 slows to call at the station with the 4.15pm train from Templecombe to Bath. Note that the locomotive now carries a double chimney, a modification undertaken at Eastleigh to a number of the class which, originally, had all been fitted with a single chimney and blastpipe. What amazed me, however, was the condition in which the permanent way was still maintained, as witnessed here and many other pictures within these pages. No wonder Ganger Jack Taylor and his team ('Gang 180' – the Midford-based p.way gang) had been awarded certificates for the high standard of permanent way maintenance in the Bristol District. The original single line from Midford to Wellow was doubled in 1892 and, until 1933, the double line extended across the viaduct as far as the signal box at the north end. *27th June 1964*

The provision of the parapet railings to the viaduct (seen here as replaced in 1958) was a specific requirement of the BoT Inspector who, having noted the proximity of the station, considered 'It is necessary that handrails of sufficient height be fixed on the tops of the parapets to prevent passengers, who might leave the carriages by mistake before reaching the platform, falling over the viaduct.' This requirement came with the doubling of the line between Midford and Wellow in 1892, not at the opening of the railway (when Midford viaduct was a much more spindly affair) some eighteen years earlier!

OPPOSITE PAGE BOTTOM: At one stage, it looked as though the Ivatt 2-6-2Ts, which had been associated with the S&D since 1949 and had proved popular with engine crews, might be eliminated from use on the line, their place being taken by the increasing use of the Collett '22/32xx' Class. This, however, did not prove to be the case and, in the latter two years when Templecombe shed came under the control of Exmouth Junction, the numbers in use on the line grew again. No. 41242, one of the original allocation to Bath in October 1949 but here based at Templecombe, sets off in the sunshine from Evercreech Junction for a leisurely run along the branch with the 5.00pm train to Highbridge. In the distance, a Down train – the 4.00pm from Highbridge – waits for the crossing gates to be opened and the starting signal to be cleared before proceeding to run around its train and set back into the middle siding. *25th July 1964*

TWO 'NINES' RETURN – ANOTHER CYNICAL PLOY?

ABOVE: For a few months during the summer of 1963, No. 92220 *Evening Star*, together with No. 92224, were transferred to Bath in response to a request for two of the BR Class '5' 4-6-0s! With no heavy through trains now running via the S&D, these two 'Nines' were an expensive and totally inappropriate choice. Perhaps, as some cynics have suggested, this was another deliberate ploy by the 'Western' to support the economic argument for closure of the S&D. I personally doubt this, the decision to close the line was, I suspect, already well entrenched in the WR policy machine. Norman's picture shows *Evening Star* waiting to leave Bath Green Park with the 1.10pm down local, comprising a lightweight load for a service which called at every station and halt all the way south to Templecombe. I recall Ivo Peters telling me how annoyed had been Mr Morris, the Shedmaster at Green Park, at having to allocate these large locomotives to such mundane tasks until such time as they could be sent packing – *Evening Star* to Cardiff, East Dock, in November 1963 and No. 92224 to Bristol in September. Ironically, in May 1964, a temporary shortage of motive power at Bath brought forth another two 'Nines' – No's 92214 and 92226 – on a short term loan arrangement. *12th September 1963*

OPPOSITE PAGE TOP: Later the same day, No. 92220 makes light work of the 1 in 50 climb towards Midsomer Norton station. Note, however, despite the WR having held responsibility for motive power since 1958, traffic still carried the old S&D headlamp code. The rails to the right were those giving access to Norton Hill Colliery, hidden from view behind the rear of the train. One of the advantages of our publisher working from Norman's original glass plate negatives is the opportunity to include detail which Norman may well have excluded from his prints. This is one such example; much of the left side of the negative would have been left out, thus denying us the distant view of the Welton end of the town of Midsomer Norton (although many locals might well argue that these are – or at least were – two very distinct communities before the growth of housing which has occurred during the past forty years). *12th September 1963*

OPPOSITE PAGE BOTTOM: Later the same month, Norman Lockett caught up with *Evening Star* again, this time at Shepton Mallet in charge of the 9.03am semi-fast service from Bristol Temple Meads (departing 9.55am from Bath Green Park) to Bournemouth West. The 'Nine' was captured drawing away from Shepton Mallet (Charlton Road) station, past the goods shed on the left and in a fortuitous juxtaposition with S&D Class '7F' No. 53807. The 2-8-0, hauling a Bath-Evercreech Junction freight, was booked a 15 minute call here, which included time to take on water. However, the freight must have been running late, so had been set back into the siding to clear the main line for the passenger train. *28th September 1963*

Sustrans have outline proposals to construct a cycleway and footpath for public use along this section of the old line, between the outskirts of Radstock and as far as Midsomer Norton station. The S&DR Heritage Trust are hoping to arrange for a 'corridor' of land to be protected in anticipation of any longer term objective to re-establish a (single) line from Midsomer Norton to Radstock.

On Bank Holidays during the summer, excursions were still sometimes provided to run from Bristol and Bath, via the S&D, to Poole and Bournemouth. On August Bank Holiday Monday in 1963, BR Class '5' No. 73054 passes Corfe Mullen Junction with the 9.30am excursion from Bath. This, again, was a very picturesque part of the line, the section from here northwards around Spetisbury often witnessing the highest speeds over the entire length of the S&D. This train had just slowed to enter the commencement of the three mile single line section to Broadstone. The other line, visible on the right, was the original route to Wimborne which, since 1933, had been truncated to act only as the access to a siding serving a local clay works. *5th August 1963*

EXCURSIONS AND SPECIALS

Another picture included to provide a reminder that the final few miles of the route between Bath and Bournemouth, southwards from Broadstone, were run over the rails of the former L&SWR. No. 73092 nears the top of the climb from east of Poole to Branksome, the severity of which appears to have done nothing to reduce the capability of the BR Class '5' to produce steam. This again was an August Bank Holiday Monday excursion, which left Bristol at 8.50am. Until the very end of such traffic, these excursions continued to prove popular and were well loaded. Notice those two leading coaches – Gresley articulated stock – and also the lineside conifers, much a feature of the Bournemouth area and from which the 'Pines Express' derived its title. *3rd August 1964*

BOURNEMOUTH WEST

The previous two views are sufficiently close to Bournemouth West to remind me that we have yet to feature this important station, the destination and starting point for S&D passenger trains. The problem is that, despite making many visits to this location, resulting in a handsome selection of photographs, for some reason Norman Lockett appears to have never pointed his camera at an S&D train! David has no knowledge of why this should be so – so this page is, of necessity, a bit of a 'cheat', in that it features SR rather than S&D line services. However, in defence, I plead that the Class 'M7' 0-4-4Ts, for so many years a feature here particularly whilst engaged on station pilot duties, would also have shunted carriage stock for traffic running via the S&D, into the platform. Further, the Bulleid 'Light Pacific' featured was destined to appear at the head of one of the 'last day' specials to traverse the S&D!

LEFT: Drummond Class 'M7' 0-4-4T No. 30127, pauses in platform No. 5 with some stock for a SR departure. This was, at the time, a regular choice of locomotive allocated to carriage shunting at Bournemouth West but, all too soon, these veterans would be withdrawn from service. *8th September 1963*

BELOW: Modified 'West Country' Class 4-6-2 No. 34013 *Okehampton* completes her journey in charge of the Sundays 10am service from Brighton. Note how the line commences to climb immediately beyond the platforms, leading towards Bournemouth West Junction, where the routes towards Poole and Bournemouth Central diverged. *9th June 1963*

As recorded a few pages earlier, withdrawal of the first of the 1925 series of S&D Class '7F' 2-8-0s occurred in December 1963. Within nine months, only one of these locomotives, No. 53807, remained in traffic. The only other ex-S&D locomotive still at work on the line was Class '4F' No. 44558. On Sunday, 7th June 1964, a special was run by the Home Counties Touring Society which used both of these two old stalwarts in tandem, the last time this would happen. The special, which ran from London to Bournemouth Central and then up the S&D to Bath, included a return run along the original S&DR main line between Evercreech Junction and Highbridge. When photographed by Norman Lockett, the train was nearing Glastonbury on the outward run, having just traversed a four mile section of the line which ran dead straight all the way from east of West Pennard station. The Somerset Levels, over which much of this part of the S&D had been built, was very different to the steeply graded and sinuous route of the main line over the Mendip Hills, which form the backdrop to this scene.

ENTHUSIASTS SPECIALS

During the final few years of the S&D, when the fate of the line had become accepted by even the most optimistic of supporters, more and more societies organised special trains, the itinerary of which included a run along at least a part of the route. Many of these have been well recorded and published for posterity so here, within the final few pages, we include just a few.

It was, perhaps, a little ironic that as the local trains attracted less and less passenger traffic (due in no small part to the growing uncertainty as to how much longer such means of travel would be possible), at weekends trainloads of enthusiasts came to visit and travel the line in ever greater numbers. In September 1965, BR Western Region published what proved to be (as far as the S&D was concerned) the last leaflets advertising the fares for 'Day Tickets' (same day Second class return fares). Today, they make interesting reading, and examples to and from Bath Green Park included Bournemouth 15s 0d (75p today – although decimal money was then still a few years away); Poole 13s 9d (69p); Glastonbury & Street 10s 3d (51p); Radstock 3s 0d (15p) and Midford 1s 7d (8p).

The 'South Western Rambler', a railtour from London organised by the Southern Counties Touring Society, arrives at Broadstone behind BR Class '9F' 2-10-0 No. 92209. The itinerary for most tours taking in the S&D usually included the northern half of the main line – what was generally referred to as 'the most interesting part'! To this extent, the SCTS special was different, visiting only the S&D southwards from Templecombe. The rear of the train is here passing over the junction which formed the southern extremity of the S&D. The final eight miles from Broadstone to Bournemouth made use of the SR route. This special, however, was proceeding to Hamworthy Junction by the original route of the Southampton & Dorchester line, which S&D trains had used to reach Lower Hamworthy, the first station for Poole. That had been a part of the S&DR's previously mentioned grandiose plan to promote a service from South Wales to France. Travelling by S&D steamer across the Bristol Channel from Cardiff to Burnham, passengers would then be taken by rail to Lower Hamworthy, for a ship to Cherbourg, allowing for onward travel by rail to Paris – a service which actually materialised for just two summers during 1865 and 1866. A direct line from Broadstone to Poole (New) was opened in December 1872, from which date S&D trains used the platforms just visible beyond the running-in station nameboard in Norman Lockett's photograph. Finally, S&D trains reached Bournemouth West when the line from Poole was extended and opened in 1874, the same year as the Evercreech to Bath line, thus creating the through route from the North of England and the Midlands to Bath and Bournemouth. *8th March 1964*

Following arrival at Hamworthy Junction, the 'South Western Rambler' reversed direction to cross Holes Bay and proceed to Bournemouth Central. 'Britannia' Class 'Pacific' No. 70020 Mercury, which had earlier brought the special from London to Salisbury, where No. 92209 took over, then returned the train to London via Southampton.

After 1964, there were no examples of the ex-Midland and LM&S Class '4F' 0-6-0s left on the S&D, although long-serving ex-S&D No. 44560 was still extant and working out of Gloucester shed. For their 'Southern Wanderer' Rail Tour, the Southern Counties Touring Society arranged for the locomotive to be 'borrowed' and return briefly to its old haunts. The special originated at London (Victoria) and ran via Bournemouth to Templecombe, where old S&D No. 60 took over for a return trip to Highbridge. The special is seen on the outward run, passing alongside the South Drain and approaching Catcott Crossing, about half a mile east of Edington Burtle. *28th March 1965*
The South Drain here had originally formed a part of the route of the Glastonbury Canal which linked that town with Highbridge and, via the River Brue, with the Bristol Channel. This canal was the waterway purchased for the construction of the Somerset Central Railway, the original part of what later became the Somerset & Dorset Railway. Here, on the day of Norman's visit, there was not the slightest wind to ripple the surface, resulting in a near-perfect mirror image of the special.

The 'Wessex Downsman Rail Tour', organised by the Locomotive Club of Great Britain, ran on the first Sunday in April 1965 and was repeated four weeks later. Commencing at Waterloo, the route was via Reading and Devizes to Bristol, then to Bath Green Park and over the S&D to Bournemouth, before returning to London. On the first occasion, with Class '8F' No. 48309 having taken over the ten-coach special at Green Park, the ascent of the two mile climb out of Bath was somewhat protracted and there was some doubt whether the summit would be reached! With progress down to slow walking speed, the top of the bank was eventually surmounted and it was subsequently discovered that some of the carriage brakes were rubbing. No such problems were encountered when the same locomotive was used for the repeat excursion, seen here, although the loading had been reduced to eight coaches. No. 48309 makes excellent progress near Wyke Champflower on the outward run to Bournemouth. This Class '8F' came to Bath from Llanelly in mid August 1964 and survived long enough to be withdrawn on closure of the S&D. *2nd May 1965*

WHIT SUNDAY AT CHILCOMPTON TUNNEL

Norman Lockett had first photographed southbound trains at this location some fifteen years earlier and subsequently returned on many occasions, yet this was the first (and only) time he crossed to the Down side of the line to obtain a picture! BR Class '5' No. 73051 bursts out of Chilcompton Tunnel with an excursion from Bath to Bournemouth West. Calling at most of the stations on the northern half of the line, this was one of two final Whit Sunday specials, the other, headed by BR Standard Class '4' No. 75009 and Class '5' No. 73054, starting from Bristol and running to a faster schedule. Both trains were reported as crowded; perhaps it was the cheap day return fare – 15 shillings (75p) from Bath. *7th June 1965*

Two final Bank Holiday excursions, also fully loaded, ran over the S&D to Poole & Bournemouth on Monday 30th August 1965. It has been recorded that these were provided by the Western Region authorities only after considerable local pressure. However, their destination at Bournemouth was the Central Station, as Bournemouth West had been closed on the 2nd August 1965. So, Norman's first ever picture from the Down side of the line at Chilcompton Tunnel also happened to feature one of the two last excursions to run to the traditional destination for S&D trains – Bournemouth West.

It's rather ironic that the 9.35am excursion, here photographed by Norman, was scheduled to take 2hrs 37mins to reach Bournemouth. Forty-three years later, the equivalent Sunday journey, the 9.27am from Bath Spa and the added inconvenience of a change of trains at Southampton Central, will get you to Bournemouth in 2hrs 56mins; that is providing there are no Sunday line occupations by Network Rail involving diversions or the ultimate 'pleasure' of transfer to a replacement bus service for a part of the journey. Such is progress! 'Slow & Dirty'? – give me the old 'Splendid & Delightful' any day.

Incidentally, whilst the decimal price of a ticket, quoted above (and elsewhere) as an aid for those less conversant with the old currency, looks cheap, it should be borne in mind that the average weekly wage in the mid 1960s was under £20, with those employed in industry and manual jobs on around half that.

FINAL FORMS OF MOTIVE POWER

A BR Class '4' 2-6-4T did not make a first foray over the S&D until late 1963. During the following two years, they were used to an ever increasing extent, proving more than adequate for the three and four coach loadings which sufficed for the declining passenger traffic. No. 80043, which was destined to remain in service and to work during the final weekend of the S&D, heads south, passing close to Wyke Champflower with the 4.13pm Evercreech Junction-Templecombe. *7th June 1965*
The signal seen here was the Up distant for Bruton Road Crossing, a little over a half-mile to the north and the first of two such road crossings – the other being Lamyatt – between here and Evercreech Junction.

Turning to look in the opposite direction, the 4.00pm Templecombe-Highbridge train, now reduced to a single coach but here with the addition of a utility van, heads northwards under Bridge No. 115 (note the plate carrying the number on the right hand abutment). Ivatt No. 41249 first arrived at Templecombe in July 1953, remaining on the S&D until early 1959. It was allocated back to Templecombe just a few weeks before this photograph was taken, remaining until closure and, as will be seen, also active on the final weekend of traffic, following which, like No. 80043, the engine was condemned for scrap. *26th June 1965*

You may recall that Norman visited the lineside at Stoney Littleton Bridge, west of Wellow, on some of his earliest outings to the S&D. This, however, is the only picture we have found looking towards the western face of the overbridge. Typifying the run-down appearance of the era shortly before closure of the line, BR Class '4' 2-6-0 No. 76026 (allocated to Bournemouth shed), is caught in the early evening sunshine whilst heading towards Shoscombe & Single Hill Halt, with the 7.05pm Bath (5.55pm ex-Bristol Temple Meads) to Bournemouth. *26th June 1965*

None of the BR Class '4' 2-6-0s were ever allocated to the S&D. No. 76026 survived to the very end of steam on the SR, withdrawn from Bournemouth in July 1967 and put into store at Weymouth awaiting scrapping. By the way, notice how the later (Up line) arch of the overbridge had to be built with a wider span than the original, to accommodate the sweep of the curve when the formation was widened for the second set of rails, brought into use between Wellow and Radstock in 1894.

A glorious autumn afternoon and, with the S&D having only a few more months to run, Norman Lockett makes what may well have been his final visit to a lineside location which had remained a firm favourite since he first photographed a train in Horsecombe Vale some thirty years earlier. The time is 3.20pm as Stanier Class '8F' 2-8-0 No. 48760 emerges from the southern portal of Combe Down Tunnel for the run down the grade across Tucking Mill Viaduct towards Midford which, like most of the smaller locations all along the line, had by now lost all facilities to handle freight traffic. Other than mineral and coal trains, the daily freight traffic was a shadow of even just a few years earlier, as this short train of vans testifies. Indeed, other than the 2.40am from Bath (the Down 'Mail', itself withdrawn from early September 1965, thus allowing the S&D to be closed each night) and the 'Perisher' (8.25pm Templecombe-Derby), no other non-passenger traffic was shown in the main Working Time Tables. All other remaining workings were now regarded and listed as Local Trip Workings in a separate WTT from 1964. By the time Norman took this photograph, even many of the traditional coal trains were – on any single weekday – 'caped' (cancelled by the Control Office). This 2-8-0 was another transfer from Llanelly, reputedly for storage at Bath but put back into traffic for just a few months. *4th October 1965*

THE 'FIRST' FINAL WEEKEND

The weekend of 1st-2nd January 1966 should have marked the end of the S&D, the last public passenger services being scheduled to run on Saturday 1st. However, as is now well recorded, because of last minute problems with one of the replacement bus services, closure was put on hold and an 'Interim Emergency Service' provided.

A new closure date, 6th March 1966, was subsequently announced with the last public services scheduled for Saturday 4th March. Meanwhile, the specials organised to run over the S&D during the original 'last weekend' were retained and further rail tours also advertised for the final 'last weekend'– demonstrating that, right to the end, the S&D was a very special line, with *two* final weekends!

On Saturday, 1st January 1966, the Locomotive Club of Great Britain ran the 'Mendip Merchantman Rail Tour'. This started from London, travelled to Bournemouth and up the S&D as far as Templecombe No. 2 Junction behind SR 'Merchant Navy' 4-6-2 No. 35011 *General Steam Navigation* **(despite this being a class officially banned from running over the S&D – but who cared about such niceties any longer!). At Templecombe, two Ivatt 2-6-2Ts, No's 41307 and 41283, were provided for a run to Highbridge and back, with No. 35011 taking over for the final leg back to London. Here, at Glastonbury – the birthplace of the Somerset Central Railway – the special waits for the last of its many passengers to rejoin the train before setting off to run along the original twelve miles of line which were destined to become a part of the Somerset & Dorset Railway.**

It may not be widely known that when the proposals for closure of the S&D were first considered, the Highbridge-Glastonbury section was excluded, a case being advanced by Western Region management to retain the single line not only for the traffic to and from the milk factory at Bason Bridge but on the basis that considerable parcels and freight traffic would continue to be generated from the Glastonbury area. Obviously much of this was dependant on the anticipated continued usage of the railway by the local shoe making, sheepskin and allied industries, the forefathers of who had been responsible for promoting the original Somerset Central Railway. However, even these proposals were rationalised to retain, until October 1972, only the short section from Highbridge to the milk factory at Bason Bridge. That year, the route was cut by the construction of the M5 motorway just to the east of Highbridge. In retrospect, what a wonderful tourist line the original twelve miles of the Somerset Central Railway would have created; a link with the Bristol-Taunton main line, a trip across the Somerset Levels (the route of the former line now bisects the Shapwick Heath Natural Nature Reserve created out of the peatlands which, for so many years, provided a major source of traffic to the branch line of the S&D) and rail access to the ever popular town of Glastonbury and, of course, its heavily attended and world renowned festival of music and performing arts held most years at nearby Pilton.

On the following day, Sunday 2nd January 1966, the Railway Correspondence & Travel Society, who planned this last day special, decided to go ahead with running their train despite the deferment of the closure. This also ran from London to Bournemouth but the change of motive power for the trip over the S&D was undertaken at Broadstone. SR 'U' Class 2-6-0 No. 31639 and 'West Country' No. 34015 *Exmouth* took control for a run all the way to Bath. A call was made at Evercreech Junction to take water and provide a 'photo stop'. Norman Lockett obtained this picture from the South Signal Box at 'the Junction' as the special approached and was about to pass over the level crossing. The organisers having eventually got all the passengers back on board following the stop for water, the special set off again for Bath. There, after a change of motive power, the rail tour continued behind Stanier '8F' No. 48309 via the Midland line to Bristol and the former GWR main line to Highbridge, where S&D metals were regained. Two Ivatt 2-6-2Ts (No's 41307 and 41283 were used again) took the train back along the branch and as far as Templecombe, ready for the final leg via Salisbury to London.

THE FINAL FINALÉ

We now move to the 'final' final weekend, the 5-6th March 1966. On the Saturday, the undoubted highlight was the LCGB special train, the 'Somerset & Dorset Rail Tour', one of two specials to be run. As with the Society's earlier 'final' rail tour, the train commenced in London, from where 'Merchant Navy' Class No. 35028 *Clan Line* brought the special via the SR West of England main line to Templecombe. From there, Ivatt 2-6-2Ts No's 41307 and 41249 took the rail tour forward to Evercreech Junction and a return journey along the Highbridge branch. Here, on the run back to 'the Junction', the two Ivatts are about to pass Stean Bow Crossing (sometimes written as 'Steanbow') to the east of West Pennard and commence the stiff climb through the woods towards Pylle. Stean Bow was one of many such remote crossings which the branch line encountered on its passage across the Somerset Levels. Most were complete with a cottage to house the crossing keeper, a lonely and mostly thankless task frequently undertaken – at least in the latter years – by the wives of permanent way or other staff.

At Evercreech Junction, two immaculately prepared Bulleid 'Light Pacifics' waited to take the special forward to Bath and then return down the S&D to Bournemouth Central, where motive power was changed a final time, with *Clan Line* taking the train back to London. In a scene reminiscent of a decade earlier when, occasionally, a pair of 'Bulleids' could be seen heading into the Georgian city in double harness, 'West Country' No. 34006 *Bude* and 'Battle of Britain' No. 34057 *Biggin Hill* forge up the long 1 in 50 gradient in fine style just north of Prestleigh Viaduct (glimpsed far right), heading towards Shepton Mallet on the northbound run to Bath.

With a little more than a mile left to complete the northbound run, *Bude* and *Biggin Hill* (the former with senior S&D driver Donald Beale in view) bring the special out of Devonshire Tunnel and sweep down the 1 in 50 gradient towards Bath Junction. Enthusiasts and photographers are evident on Maple Grove Bridge, although many more would assemble to see the return run of the two 'Bulleids' which, apparently, made a very impressive ascent of Devonshire Bank as a prelude to a similar speedy climb of the Mendips!

The afternoon sunshine of a sad late winter Saturday highlights BR Class '4' 2-6-4T No. 80043 in charge of the 16.25pm from Green Park, the last southbound public train to depart Bath during daylight hours. Heading away from Wellow, it was a case of 'standing room only', the three coaches being inadequate for such an important event. However, no strengthening of the last day public services had been permitted, other than where it was a convenient means of clearing any remaining stock away from the line. In contrast to the opening day and the passage of the first train, it was, perhaps, unsurprising that on this occasion, ninety-two years later, no bells tolled from St Julian's Church to mark the sad demise of the S&D. *5th March 1966*

THE LAST TWO SPECIALS

Farewell to the Former
Somerset and Dorset Joint Railway

Photo: I. Peters.   Block Courtesy: Railway Magazine.
53807, the (then) sole survivor of the S.D.J.R. class 7F 2-8-0s at Masbury summit
with the 8.55 a.m. down freight from Bath on the last day of its service, 5th
September, 1962.

Photographic Souvenir

in connection with

LAST PASSENGER TRAIN

on the

Bath — Templecombe — Bournemouth Section

SUNDAY, 6th MARCH, 1966

Organised by the STEPHENSON LOCOMOTIVE SOCIETY
(Midland Area)

ABOVE: And so, to the very last day – Sunday 6th March 1966. Unlike the previous day, the weather was overcast, a reflection perhaps of a very sad occasion. Two specials were run, one by the Railway Correspondence & Travel Society, the other by the Midland Area of the Stephenson Locomotive Society (who produced a commemorative photographic souvenir leaflet, LEFT). The SLS Special made a run from Bath to Bournemouth Central* and back. The previous day, No. 48706 had run, unassisted, with a special organised by the Great Western Society. The lack of any steam heating was, apparently, unappreciated! Accordingly, the following day, for this train, BR Class '4' 2-6-4T No. 80043 was 'tucked inside' No. 48706 for this very purpose. Here, the train speeds southwards through Cole, less than a mile from the point where, 104 years earlier, the Somerset Central and the Dorset Central railways had met, end to end, to create the Somerset & Dorset Railway. Before the beginning of 1966, Cole had already been denuded of all signals, its signal box and the small goods yard, the site of the latter here hidden by the exhaust from both locomotives. All too soon, the two running lines would be ripped up and, many years later, a small housing development would obliterate the original trackbed of this once proud cross-country railway at this point.

As mentioned a few pages earlier, Bournemouth West, the traditional terminus of through S&D passenger traffic since 1874, had been closed (supposedly on a temporary basis) on 2nd August 1965, since which date S&D trains had been diverted to the Central station or terminated at Branksome.

The RCTS Special, featured OPPOSITE RIGHT, commenced at Waterloo and, because of Sunday engineering works, ran via Staines Central, Woking, Aldershot, Alton and Winchester to reach Bournemouth and Broadstone, then along the S&D as far as Templecombe Junction. The motive power for this leg, as on the previous day with the LCGB train, was 'Merchant Navy' 4-6-2 No. 35028 Clan Line. From Templecombe Junction, the special was taken over by Ivatt 2-6-2Ts No's 41283 and 41249 for the run to Evercreech Junction and along the branch to Highbridge. There, the train was transferred to the WR main line, where Modified 'West Country' Class No. 34013 Okehampton took over. The next leg of the trip ran to Bristol and to Mangotsfield North Junction. There, the train reversed direction, running to Bath Green Park behind 'Hymek' diesel No. D7014, whilst No. 34013 followed so as to take over for the southbound leg across the Mendips.

At Bath, the RCTS Special was taken over by No. 34013 *Okehampton* **and a second Bulleid, No. 34057** *Biggin Hill*, **was tucked inside to provide this impressive combination of motive power for the very last passenger train to depart Green Park and run southbound over the S&D, as far as Templecombe. There the special was again reversed and No. 35028 attached to return the train to Waterloo.**

It is perhaps appropriate to me that Norman Lockett took his final photograph of the S&D at Midford, the place where I first 'discovered' the line and spent more than a little of my time in the 1950s and up until early 1965. As neither locomotive was fitted with an automatic exchanger, the tablet was carried in a large pouch. The special made a stop (unplanned?) to enable signalman Percy Savage to retrieve the single line tablet and, perhaps, to remind both drivers that the train would be halted and reversed at Writhlington, to run 'wrong line' as far as Midsomer Norton – the Down line already having been broken at Radstock and slewed to create a connection with the former North Somerset line, to enable coal to continue to be taken out from Writhlington Colliery. Photographs of this leg of the journey have featured much less than others as, from Midford southwards, what little daylight remaining soon started to fade. However, with such an abundance of motive power for a nine coach train, it was reported that the crews of both locomotives were determined the S&D would 'go out in style'. Thus followed what has been claimed to be the fastest ever ascent from Midsomer Norton to Masbury Summit.

Midford Viaduct, forty-two years after that final train pulled away, as viewed from a vantage point as near as is possible to where Norman Lockett took his last ever S&D photograph. Other than the skyline and the parapet railings to the left, the only other point of reference between the two views is the chimney pot of the house once occupied by Midford signalman Percy Savage – the chimney seen smoking above the photographer in the 1966 view, which can just be seen beyond the parapet railings, in a line drawn immediately above the dog in this 2008 scene. The present viewpoint differs because all that foliage on the left obscures the view from Norman's position, whilst the formation level is also lower but the family here enjoying a walk across the viaduct have reached the spot which corresponds almost exactly with the rear of the tender of No. 34013 overleaf. By the way, just a word of warning to dog walkers. As this family were about to discover, dogs are not allowed along the pathway towards Wellow from a point just behind the camera position here! *MJA/31st May 2008*

Following closure of the line, the former trackbed over Midford Viaduct, with access barred at both ends, became overgrown and even sported a number of silver birch trees. Then, in 2006, a scheme was approved to open up the old route from Midford almost as far as Wellow. This was part of a project managed by Sustrans, being a short but significant section of the cycle and walking route from Dundas Aqueduct (in the Limpley Stoke Valley), via Monkton Combe, Midford and Wellow, to Radstock and then onwards to Frome. Named 'The Colliers Way', this now forms part of National Cycle Route 24. More recently, in early 2008, partial funding was awarded by the National Lottery for 'The Two Tunnels Scheme', a bold and exciting project, which will reopen the S&D route – for use by cyclists and walkers – between Bath and Midford, including Devonshire and Combe Down tunnels, both of which will be illuminated. Preparatory work started in March 2008. Details can be found at www.twotunnels.org.uk

SOMERSET AND DORSET JOINT LINE.
TRESPASSING ON THE RAILWAY.

NOTICE IS HEREBY GIVEN THAT UNDER THE PROVISIONS OF THE 37TH SECTION OF THE SOUTH WESTERN RAILWAY ACT, 1902, ANY PERSON WHO SHALL TRESPASS UPON ANY OF THE LINES OF RAILWAY BELONGING OR LEASED TO OR WORKED BY THE SOUTH WESTERN RAILWAY COMPANY IN CONJUNCTION WITH THE MIDLAND RAILWAY COMPANY, SHALL ON CONVICTION BE LIABLE TO A PENALTY NOT EXCEEDING 40/- & PUBLIC WARNING IS HEREBY GIVEN TO PERSONS NOT TO TRESPASS UPON THE RAILWAY.

DATED THIS 5TH DAY OF AUGUST 1903
GODFREY KNIGHT,
WILLIAM CLOWER,
} JOINT SECRETARIES.

Beyond Radstock, the S&DR Heritage Trust is beginning to make progress towards restoring the first short section of railway southwards beyond their station base at Midsomer Norton. Sustrans is looking, longer term, to gain access to other sections of the old trackbed beyond Radstock. An enthusiast has purchased Masbury station and intends to restore the site to its former glory (but not for public access). At Henstridge, the narrow gauge Gartell Railway runs, in part, along the trackbed of the S&D whilst at Stalbridge, Sturminster Newton, Shillingstone to Blandford, and Charlton Marshall to Spetisbury, sections of the old Dorset Central end of the line form the 'North Dorset Trailway'. Finally, also at Shillingstone, the station and its environs are now the headquarters of the North Dorset Steam Trust, with restoration of the buildings, platform and trackbed generally completed. There's life in the old S&D yet!